To Doneen,
Fro

1952

The
YOUNG QUEEN
The Life Story of
HER MAJESTY QUEEN ELIZABETH II

Godfrey Winn

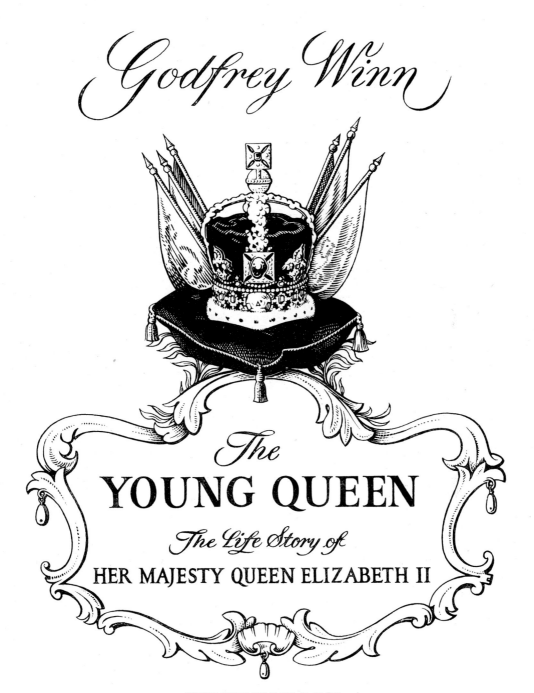

The
YOUNG QUEEN
The Life Story of
HER MAJESTY QUEEN ELIZABETH II

HUTCHINSON

1952

DESIGNED BY

Robert Talbot Bodle

Made and
Printed in Great Britain
by the
HUTCHINSON PRINTING
TRUST LIMITED

Dedicated to

all the

inheritors of the

New

Elizabethan Era

The Young Queen

ALL OF US have our own particular, our own private picture in our mind of the princess who has so recently become our Queen. The impression may change as she herself has changed from being simply her father's daughter, dedicated to the same destiny, to being the wife of a sailor, and the mother of two children of her own: but for my own part there is one picture of the Queen, captured upon the screen of my consciousness (and some months before her Accession), that will remain in my memory as long as life itself.

Till that moment, when it happened, I had always thought of her as I had seen her, magnificent in her scarlet riding habit, taking the salute, in her father's place, at the Trooping the Colour, on a shining June morning, when the moving frieze of men and horses in the foreground, so brilliantly accoutred, so beautifully ordered, and the fresh verdancy of St. James' Park in the background, made a panorama so unmistakably English that it caught at one's heart and one's imagination. But that summer of 1951, as all summers, had to pass, and it

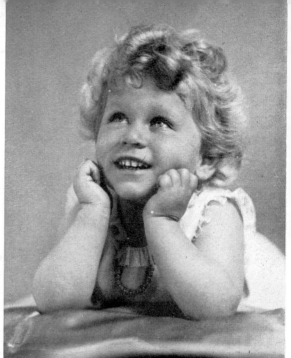

Aged two

Aged five, with her mother

was almost autumn when I saw Princess Elizabeth, as she then was, for the last time before she set out on her Canadian mission of goodwill. It was a Saturday night at a cinema in Leicester Square. Not a private visit, as she and her husband often liked to make, before they lived at Buckingham Palace, and were not showing a new film themselves to a few friends in their own projection theatre, fitted up in the basement of Clarence House.

No, this was an official visit: she was there to do a job. In consequence, she was dressed in bright satin and sequins to look once more like the fairy princess in the fable. The occasion was the first performance of Anna Neagle's interpretation of Florence Nightingale in *The Lady with a Lamp*: one more charity gala, this time in aid of a school for nursing. Every seat in the theatre had been sold, some at ten times their value, not so much because of the worthiness

Aged six

of the cause but because, to use once more that stock, familiar phrase, Royalty was to be present.

Yes, but would Royalty be present? That was the question mark in most minds right up to the last moment. The papers had been so full of the preparations at Buckingham Palace for the operation that was to be performed on the King that weekend. That night? Supposing the surgeons had fixed the operation for that evening? Would the Duke and Duchess of Edinburgh still come? Would he come without her?

And then all speculation ended as the trumpets sounded and down the aisle of the circle came the royal procession, headed by the King's elder daughter, with a tiara like a crown upon her head, and instead of a sceptre, a great bunch of white carnations and roses in her arms. She stood there, acknowledging her reception, smiling and composed, as though she hadn't a care in the world.

Aged seven, with her father

She really was radiant. That is a much-misused adjective, but those of us who were close enough could truly sense the aura of radiance that surrounded her. And marvel at it. Most of all, marvel at the way that she did not falter, even at the end of the performance, when once again the trumpets blew and the Guards' band struck up the National Anthem, and upon the screen was thrown the coloured image of King George VI, dressed in the uniform of a Marshal of the R.A.F., with his face still young and unscarred by pain.

Happy and Glorious,
Long to reign over us,
God Save the King.

The playing seemed as long as eternity that evening, and all the time his daughter stood there, so straight and still, gazing out at her father's carved head.

Yet it was not difficult to imagine what must have been in her mind, what thoughts of the hungry generations treading her down, though she showed no trace, even then, of sadness or dismay. Instead, she left the theatre as she had arrived, still smiling with the sweetness and the courage of her youth.

Such is the picture eternally in my mind (and more so than ever now with the Coronation of Elizabeth the Second so soon ahead of her) and often, too, I find my thoughts returning to an afternoon, eight years ago now, when I had the privilege of being received in King George VI's own sitting room, on the first floor at Buckingham Palace.

My hostess on that occasion was one of the Queen Mother's ladies-in-waiting, Lady Delia Peel, and we sat there, talking about Princess Elizabeth—the official reason for my visit, as a writer—in the two armchairs usually occupied by her parents. But of all the intimate and revealing details that I was entrusted with that afternoon, the part of the conversation that has stayed most vividly of all in my memory ever since was that given over to an account of how the future Queen of England conquered an agonizing attack of nerves one morning when she was seventeen.

It was the morning when she set forth from her war-time home at Windsor Castle, to drive to Salisbury Plain, where she was to perform her first "grown-up" inspection of a battalion of the Grenadier Guards whose honorary colonel she had just become, and whose crest in diamonds she wore upon the lapel of her teen-age coat.

In the car, Lilibet kept on looking down at the badge, as though it was a star, but it didn't help much! What should she do with her bag during the march past? A hundred questions tormented her. Finally, the elderly woman at her side, who had spent a lifetime walking behind her royal mistress at official functions, had a brain-wave.

"Do you know what I did, Mr. Winn?" Lady Delia exclaimed to me that afternoon in Buckingham Palace. "I fished in my bag and found the last of my sweet ration. Barley sugar. I gave it to the Princess. Munch it slowly, I told her. You'll find it is very good for the stomach muscles."

Now they used to make an issue of glucose to us in our ship as a war-time remedy for seasickness. And, on this occasion, at any

EARLY FAMILY
SNAPSHOTS

Queen Mary takes her grandchildren to the Trooping the Colour, 1933

rate, the formula worked. For the young girl, in her simple tweed coat, walked up and down between the lines of soldiers as though she had been inspecting troops all her days. The whole battalion marched past twice, but she never moved.

Her first ordeal was over . . . and I imagined the anecdote to be over, too. But it wasn't, quite. There was a postscript, a rather significant postscript for any would-

be historian. As the royal party drove towards home again, and the honorary colonel was able to relax at last, a happy and triumphant schoolgirl, they passed Stonehenge, in the distance.

The Princess was enchanted by her first glimpse of it. "But we couldn't stop," the lady-in-waiting added on a final note. "We couldn't stop, even to have a private view of Stonehenge. It wasn't on the

adored with an almost maternal affection.

I was immensely struck on the two occasions when Princess Margaret has spoken to me of her sister of the way that her own expression changed, not so much in love, as in wonder, in the same way that anyone's face will change, speaking of a fellow pilgrim, whose future is already dedicated: or of an experience somehow tinged with mysticism.

I use that comparison deliberately. For Princess Elizabeth there was always a mystical quality attached to the throne that has now with tragic suddenness become hers. And her certain knowledge of this has already proved a source of immense strength to her, helping her not only to overcome fatigue and staleness, during the ever-increasing programme she has to fulfil, but also to overcome the nervous shyness that harried her father throughout his lifetime.

The essential service of Royalty in the modern world, it has been said, is to provide the symbols upon which a nation can nourish the sense of its own greatness. Our young Queen is very much aware of that challenge to her quality, and she feels her dedication to the throne, and all that such a dedication implies, as deeply as any noviciate on the threshold of taking her vows.

But, in fact, the Princess who became heir apparent at such a defencelessly youthful age, and is soon to be crowned in Westminster Abbey with all the pomp and ceremony of medieval custom, has already taken hers. Do you remember the broadcast that Elizabeth made on her twenty-first birthday, when she was with her parents

schedule." She was only seventeen, but already, in a way, "the prison gates" were closing fast. Not that she herself minded. Or rather, not that she herself did not understand. Right from the beginning, right from her childhood, as I hope to show in subsequent chapters, our young Queen seems to have appreciated to an extraordinary degree that her destiny was apart, even from that of the younger sister whom she

13

touring South Africa? During the tour, they almost lived in trains, and the evening before her broadcast, the King's Private Secretary, meeting her in the corridor, near Bloemfontein, asked her what she thought of the first draft that had been submitted to her, for her approval.

"It has made me cry," said the Princess simply. And she meant that, not sentimentally, but because she had been so sincerely moved by the message that she would tomorrow have the chance of delivering, in her clear, unaffected voice, so like her mother's, to twenty million people. This was the message:

"I declare before you all that my whole life, whether it be long or short, shall be devoted to your service, and the service of our great Imperial family to which we all belong.

"But I shall not have strength to carry out this resolution unless you join in it with me, as I now invite you to do: I know that your support will be unfailingly given. God help me to make good my vow, and God bless all of you who are willing to share it."

Words of a broadcast, shaped by other hands. It is easy to be cynical and dismiss it as lip-service: not so easy, however, if one has the opportunity to go behind the scenes,

Studio Lisa

to watch the royal performance from the other side of the footlights: to see what is really behind the façade.

Of course, Life, least of all for Royalty, never stands still. And that realization may well have been in the Princess's own mind, when in the August of 1951 she and her husband stayed with Earl and Countess Mountbatten of Burma, for a ball they were giving at their Romsey home, to celebrate the coming of age of their second daughter, Pamela. Since was it not to Broadlands that the Duke had brought his bride on the first part of their honeymoon?

She had been twenty-one herself then,

with her broadcast, her declaration of faith, only a few months behind her, and now four years later she was a young matron with two children of her own, though there was certainly nothing of the young matron look about her that night. Indeed, it would not be an exaggeration to say that her appearance was transformed, just as the house itself was transformed from the last time I had stayed there.

That night the eighteenth-century façade with its sculptured pillars at the entrance was floodlit, and the phosphorescent glow seemed to stretch right down to the waters of the river, pin-pricking like moths, the

WEEK-ENDS AT ROYAL LODGE, WINDSOR

passing figures of the dancers, as they hovered by the fountains, or smoked a cigarette under the trees. A magical evening, for though Broadlands is always beautiful, in all seasons, all weathers, the floodlighting had added an almost unearthly glamour: whereas the transformation in the personality of the Princess had little to do with the richness of her pink dress to the creating of which yards and yards of tulle had gone, or to the necklace of rubies, worth a ransom.

No, it was something much deeper than that (for had not one seen her in fabulous court dresses before?), more fundamental even than the fact that she had clearly lost a considerable amount of weight, and had a new coiffure, with her hair much closer to the shape of her head, and much less of it, too, it seemed.

Yet though she danced every dance that evening, never once did I see her put her hand to her hair, or take out a mirror to look at her make-up. She had a new poise, a new sense of confidence, most noticeable, even in that assembly of elegant and lovely women: the poise and confidence that someone has who is truly happy, truly loved.

All evening, in whichever part of the long drawing-room she danced, even if the centre archway divided them, always as her partner turned, so did her eyes turn, too, to watch her husband, with tender affection.

And I found myself thinking: now her goodness is matched with *his* good sense. It is *his* influence that has brought about this metamorphosis from a pretty, plumpish girl into a great beauty, who would be acclaimed anywhere. Clearly she believes that to be a good Queen for the rest of her days, she must be a good wife now, this and

every moment. She must be willing, in her private life, to be guided by the strength and knowledge he possesses through having inhabited a man's world.

Consequently, that evening at Broadlands, many other guests, besides myself, remarked that they felt that they were seeing their future Queen for the first time. Millions of others, among the King's subjects, were to have the same reaction, though to a greater degree, when a few weeks later the dazzling series of pictures appeared of her, highlighting her triumphant progress through Canada, when she was acclaimed with almost religious fervour. Not simply for what she represented, but for herself.

And it was then that the full realization came to me of all that had happened in the years since that afternoon in her childhood home, when I had been told about the barley sugar, and I found suddenly that I had a great desire to turn back the pages of her personal scrapbook right to the day of her birth.

After all, I reminded myself, more than a quarter of a century had elapsed since that day. Broadlands might be full of history, full of the memories of the time when Florence Nightingale came there as a girl, and Lord Palmerston wrote his speeches standing at the reading-desk in the library, but heaven knows, this last quarter of a century has been full of history, too.

A whole new generation has been born and grown up, since that moment when King George VI had found himself, unexpectedly, crowned King. This generation could only know the pictures of our Queen as she is today, emerging from Royal mourning, proceeding with infinite serenity

Taken at home in the last days of peace, 1939

bout her ceremonial tasks, or at home with er children, and her husband at her side. What of the years when she herself was a child? How fascinating for us all (and that what I intend to try to do during the ext few chapters) to trace the growth and he development both in character and in earing, right from the start, up to that moment of the pre-dawn of a new Eliza-ethan age, which is crystallized by a cutting om the correspondence columns of *The ̄imes*.

After the visit of the Duke and Duchess of Edinburgh to Washington, a citizen of that other capital, across the water, wrote:

"I cannot believe that such a little girl can possess such quiet strength and serenity. This cannot be all trained in her: there is something deeper, God-given, I believe. She will be great in the years to come, because of this sweetness and humility, which accompanies keen intelligence and perception."

Yes, but how did it all start? How did it all begin?

Spectators at the Lyceum Pantomime

CHAPTER TWO

APRIL is traditionally a happy month in our country. It is the time of the Easter Festival, when there is a feeling of rebirth everywhere, with a profusion of spring flowers competing in park and cottage gardens while, most pleasant reminder, the sun begins once more to possess sufficient warmth to herald another summer just over the horizon.

But the April of 1926 was rather different; there was a bitter coldness in the air; the bitterness of acute party strife, of an industrial deadlock that was to culminate in the General Strike, when all public service came to a standstill for the first and last time, one hopes, in the history of these islands, and deep, brooding bitternesses were brought to the surface to leave scars unhealed for many years to come.

How strangely ironic it seems that this should have been the moment chosen by Destiny for the arrival of the child who one day would reign over us as our Queen! Can some symbolic connection be traced between the two events, so close in time, so closely linked in their different ways to the future well-being of the whole populace? Whatever the possible portents the facts are clear enough. On the twenty-first of April of that year at No. 17 Bruton Street, which lies just off Berkeley Square, a first child was born to the Duchess of

York, at three o'clock in the morning.

In accordance with ancient custom, since discarded, the Home Secretary of the day, Sir William Joynson Hicks, was present that night in the house which, belonging to the Duchess's parents, the Strathmores, was later to be destroyed by a bomb during an air raid. History does not relate what Sir William said when he had the privilege of being the first outsider to gaze upon the baby, but it is recorded that the next day when its paternal grandparents drove from Buckingham Palace to inspect their first grandchild, born the fourth lady in the

Participants in a very different kind of Pageant. Coronation 1937

land, Queen Mary exclaimed as she bent over the cot: 'I wish you were more like your little mother. . . .'

In looks, in character? Later the child was to show herself to be in a dozen different ways every inch her father's daughter, and right from the start it was clear that she had inherited from the male side of her family the intense, deep-rooted shyness which made her howl lustily at her christening when she was confronted by so many strange, staring eyes. They could anoint her with Holy water brought specially from the River Jordan, and dress her in the same historic robe of Brussels lace that was already hallowed by other royal christenings, still there was only one thing that would comfort her on her very first public appearance, and that was the bribe of the bottle tucked in her nanny's arms. Her future training in how to suffer in silence on all occasions had not yet begun.

However, for Elizabeth Alexandra Mary, as she was christened that May afternoon by the Archbishop of Canterbury in the chapel at Buckingham Palace, it was to begin soon enough. For early in the New Year her parents had to leave her for five months to make a royal tour of Australia so as to be present when Canberra became the new capital of the Dominion. Twenty-five years later, almost to the day, it looked as though history was to repeat itself when this time the Duke and Duchess of Edinburgh set out to make the same journey, again representing the King, but on this occasion, there were two small children to be left behind in the charge of nannies, who did not expect to see their Royal mistress again before the spring and summer were over.

Life-saving exercise at the Bath Club

Of course, there is nothing quite like the British nanny: an institution which is regarded with awe and wonder the whole world over. Certainly there could not have been a finer example of this noble, if sometimes intimidating breed than the Hertfordshire woman, Miss Knight, who had been the Duchess of York's own nanny and who was later to be christened by Lilibet her own beloved Alah.

In her turn, Alah could do anything she liked with the child, and there was no safer pair of hands in England. All the same, there was the parting, there was the wrench, and on the day before they had to leave, the child's mother, as a kind of talisman, clasped round her baby's throat her first piece of jewellery: a simple necklace of coral beads that is to be noticed in most of the early childhood pictures. And now today, whenever I see the Queen in public wearing one of her magnificent diamond chains—for they are like chains of office—I find myself wondering how soon it will be before we shall see a picture of Princess Anne wearing her mother's corals: one more link in another kind of chain.

As in the case of a multitude of other children, during her parents' enforced absence, the Strathmores shared the pleasure of looking after their grandchild with her other pair of grandparents who lived at Buckingham Palace. And when it was the child's turn to go there, she would be brought down at tea time every afternoon, in a clean dress with a blue sash, and Queen Mary would hold out her arms with a delighted cry: "Here comes the Bambino."

Whereupon Lilibet would advance across the floor to her grandmother's lap, not crawling as most babies do, lying close to the floor, but sitting upright on one leg, and then scuttling vigorously with the other. Right from the very beginning, it is reported that she showed great independence of spirit, eager for the moment when she could stand alone, on her own feet.

She could, indeed, stand to greet her parents on their return, presenting them, in exchange for all the toys and presents showered upon them by the Australian people, with two words of which she was rightly extremely proud, for were they not her very own version of "Mummie" and "Papa"? Which, it is not without interest to note, are the same parental names that both she and her sister still used up to their father's death.

Lilibet was a placid child who loved to smile, especially at dogs, though already in her very blue eyes the grown-ups would surprise a solemn, wondering look as though she was trying to puzzle out what it all meant: especially the crowds that gathered so mysteriously to watch her take her daily airing in the park, now that her family had moved to their new home at No. 145 Piccadilly.

Her parents could do everything in their power to make her childhood follow a normal course. They could give her a toy tricycle for her third birthday, and a Shetland pony the next year, and her own privy purse that she could produce with a flourish from her own small blue handbag, in a shop at Forfar, announcing with glee on her return: "Oh, Alah, look what I bought with my own money."

Yes, all who were in the conspiracy could pretend that pennies must be saved up for special occasions, they could pretend in a hundred other ways, such as dressing her throughout her childhood in the simplest of clothes, nevertheless the fact remained—inescapable, insurmountable—that, apart from their adored summer holidays at Glamis Castle, where later it was to be the greatest pleasure of the two young sisters to stretch chewing-gum between the lines and watch from the railway platform what happened when the express roared through, only once in those very early years was this child of great destiny able to build her own castles in the sand, in the carefree manner of other children.

This was when she was chosen to be her grandfather's close companion and rallying force during his stay on the south coast after his very severe illness at the close of 1928. That next spring, Lilibet played to her heart's content upon the sands, with only a detective guarding her safety from a discreet distance, and in return, in gratitude for her momentary freedom, she christened the omnipotent being (who, in his turn, also in gratitude, had renamed the town of his convalescence, Bognor Regis) Grandpapa England.

There are several legendary accounts of the bestowing of that royal nickname, which will echo down the corridors of Time, but this is the authentic one; just as there are many legendary stories of Lilibet's childhood, like the one, much bandied about at one moment, of the imperious little madam who, not satisfied that she was getting sufficient attention in her own domain at the top of the house, lifted the telephone that was connected to the lower regions and called out sharply: "Royalty speaking".

The Princess has no memory today of that incident for the simple reason that it did not happen. Not only was such a display alien to her character, it did not go, either, with the very simple atmosphere of her home. On the other hand, what the Princess does remember vividly from those far-off days of more than twenty years ago, was her first visit to the Royal Tournament at Olympia.

She was just four, and the whole afternoon was ecstasy; at least, it was as soon as she grew used to the salvoes of gunfire. The first sent her scurrying out of the box, into Alah's arms: the second made her bury her head in Queen Mary's lap: but by the third she was becoming acclimatized, so that by the time the Ladder and Rope Climbing display was in progress, her excitement was so great that she almost fell over the edge of the box, and was only clutched and pulled back just in time by the Duke of Gloucester.

However, Lilibet recovered her balance sufficiently to give a special salute to the troops lined up in front of the royal party. A perfect imitation of her elders. It was no more than that yet.

One afternoon that same summer driving in Hyde Park with her mother, she asked for the first time the question that her family had been dreading. Why did everyone wave their handkerchiefs and raise their hats towards her? "Because you are a little princess," her mother answered simply.

"Were you a princess when you were small?" her daughter continued unexpectedly. Whereupon the Duchess explained that she had received royal rank through marrying a prince of royal blood. "Then if

In her Girl Guide uniform she
registers at a Labour Exchange
on her sixteenth birthday

As a Girl Guide she enjoyed
every moment of her training

I grow up and marry a man will he be a prince because I am a princess?" Lilibet persisted. "No, dear, not necessarily," her mother replied tactfully, thus leaving her daughter still wondering . . . but still waving to the crowds at the roadside.

The child's growing sense of her own importance, her awareness of a future destiny remote from that of other children, was momentarily obliterated late that summer by an event far more exciting than her visit to the Royal Tournament. This happened on the twenty-first day of August, 1930.

All day a great storm had been brewing and encircling the ancient turrets of Glamis Castle, so that it was almost a relief when the threat became a reality. Now the night was made brilliant as day by fantastic flashes of lightning preceded inevitably by harsh, reiterant thunder, which to the watchers and the waiting villagers was like so many rolls upon the drum that was to herald a new entrance upon the royal scene.

All through that night, and during the next day, a great host of well-wishers gathered outside the castle walls, and they were rewarded at last, when the weather abated, by the sight of bonfires, lit in celebration on the encircling hills, and by a glimpse of Princess Elizabeth, held up by Alah, at a window.

She wanted to see the bonfires, too; but most of all she wanted to see her new baby sister, and when she did, it is said that her first reaction was to name her 'Bud', adding, in explanation, that she wasn't a real rose yet, only a bud.

A pretty tale? Certainly later to be a pretty bud: but even more certainly can it be stated that never once, not even at the beginning, did the elder sister show the least sign of resentment or jealousy that her sole position in the family had now been assailed. On the contrary, Lilibet at once assumed a maternal and proprietary air in regard to the newcomer that has lasted even unto today, when her younger sister has come of age and gives many proofs of being entirely capable of making up her own mind on all occasions.

Of course, in the early days they squabbled sometimes, as all families do. The elder sister had a fierce temper, when finally provoked, but such outbursts did need a great deal of provoking and never lasted long nor did she ever sulk, for that was entirely alien to her early acceptance of her life with its inexorable timetable.

For already by the time she was seven the elder sister was spending several hours in her nursery every day with her governess, Crawfie, who fast was usurping in her affections the place previously given to Alah. Still, Alah did not mind, for had she not now a new baby to watch over all day long?

Miss Crawford was most suitably a Scottish girl from Dunfermline, who, after studying at a training college in Edinburgh, had planned a career as a child psychologist. Instead, she was persuaded by the charm of Lilibet's mother to devote the next seventeen years of her life to instructing the heir to the throne of England in many other things beside the French, English, arithmetic, history and geography that were the first subjects to be tackled under the glass dome of No. 145 Piccadilly.

As for her first meeting with her future pupil, Miss Crawford has herself described

in one of her own books, how she arrived in London to find a small figure with a mop of fair curls sitting up in bed. Lilibet had had her bath and now she wore a nightie with a design of small roses on it, while she had tied the cords of her dressing-gown to the knobs of her bed and was most intently driving her team of imaginary horses.

"Do you usually drive in bed?" the visitor asked politely.

"I mostly go once or twice round the park before I go to sleep. You see, it exercises my horses," she explained with pride and affection in her voice. For horses were the first love of her life, and, after her family, still are today. While Owen, her groom, was the most wonderful man in the world. So much so that on one occasion, when she asked her father a question, he replied briefly: "Why ask me? Why not ask Owen? I thought he knew everything."

Great was her delight when on her seventh birthday into the courtyard of Windsor Castle Owen led Peggy, a far larger pony than she had ever had before, but, before disappearing in the direction of the park with her favourite in attendance, Lilibet insisted on her baby sister being lifted on to the saddle and leading her round the courtyard, as her own birthday treat.

That was a spontaneous gesture, and, though it may seem a tiny incident, it has a significance in the story I have to tell of a girl born to be Queen who might so easily have become insufferably spoilt and self-centred had it not been for the innate goodness of her character.

Of course, today, goodness by many is considered to be rather a dull virtue, as old-fashioned and dated as Victorian art.

Instead, very modern parents prefer their offspring to be precocious and sophisticated from an early stage, for even when that means constant tantrums and childish displays of temperament, it may also disclose, here and there, touches of brilliance, if not genius.

It must be admitted straight away that there were no such flashes of brilliance, either in conversation or in brain power, in Lilibet's make-up. Indeed, had she been sent away to boarding-school, as most other girls in her sphere, her headmistress would have truthfully been able to record on her report that Elizabeth Alexandra Mary was conscientious, industrious and universally popular with everyone because of her pleasant manners. In fact, she was at that stage the plodding type, saved from dullness by the sweetness of her disposition, but entirely lacking the mercurial interludes that were to be produced at a surprisingly early stage in her development by Margaret Rose.

On the other hand, whereas the baby of the family surrounded herself with a mess wherever she went, the elder sister was immensely neat and tidy; so much so that she confesses herself that she would climb out of bed again to see if she had put her shoes together in their proper place. However, let me hasten to add that she never gave herself superior airs, either for her domestic virtues, or for her four years' seniority. Instead, she was perfectly happy to share all her toys with Margaret Rose, even to the Winnie the Pooh books that their adored Uncle David (then Prince of Wales) gave them each Christmas.

And, let it be put on record, they also

shared one fault much frowned upon by grown-ups. They bit their nails, and they went on biting them, despite a joint campaign launched by Alah and Crawfie that had a considerable setback on the occasion when the two little princesses, with a devilish clarity of gaze, at some public function, spotted no less a personage than Mr. Chamberlain biting his! So they returned home triumphantly to demand; if the Prime Minister could bite his nails, why couldn't they be allowed to bite *theirs*?

Their governess does not relate what satisfactory answer she was able to produce for this conundrum, but it must have been a source of considerable relief for her when about this time the children's grandmother, Queen Mary, began to take a strong and practical interest in their education and upbringing.

Lilibet's parents were so happy in each other's company, so happy when they came upstairs after tea and indulged in games of Racing Demon and pillow fights, that they were eager to leave well alone, but Queen Mary had other views about what should go into childish heads.

Did they ever learn poetry by heart? An excellent memory-trainer for the future. Would it not be better to do less arithmetic and more history, at least where Princess Elizabeth was concerned? And did they know the Bible as well as they should?

Their grandmother did not only put forward suggestions: firmly she took over the reins herself sometimes. A message would be delivered over the telephone, suggesting that as Her Majesty was going to visit a certain museum or exhibition that afternoon, it might be a good arrangement

She plays the Queen in pantomime

for, at any rate, her elder granddaughter to accompany her. Everyone accepted the telephone message as a royal command!

All the same, the little princesses began to look forward to these outings, when they trotted behind that majestic figure in the toque that was more truly regal than any coronet, for Granny always knew so much about everything, and always the best things to see, and never minded how many questions they asked.

So, altogether, the expeditions to such places as the Science Museum at South Kensington, or the Victoria and Albert, would turn out to be as exciting in a different way as their visit to the Lyceum pantomime;

or their very first and only excursion on the Underground, when they travelled from St. James' Park to Tottenham Court Road and ended up by having tea at the Y.W.C.A. there.

On one occasion, Queen Mary had taken her elder granddaughter to a concert in the Queen's Hall. Long before the end of the performance, Lilibet had begun to wriggle in her seat, as small children have a habit of doing. Would she like to go home? "Oh no," the Princess is supposed to have replied. "We can't leave before the end. Think, Granny, of all the people waiting to see us outside."

The Queen's reply was to turn to her

LEFT: *"Old Mother Red Riding Boots,"*
Windsor Castle, Christmas 1944

lady-in-waiting and command her to take the Princess out by the back way and home in a taxi. Although they could not stop her from being conscious—over-conscious in fact—sometimes of her royal inheritance, they could try to keep the future, and its implacable demands, at bay for as long as possible.

Until there came that day early in the January of 1936 when Princess Elizabeth was playing on the lawns at Sandringham. She and her sister were just putting the finishing touches to a snowman, when they found their grandmother at their side. She did not try to stop them playing. because

they were only children, but she did break the news to them that Grandpapa England was ill, very ill indeed. And after lunch that day Queen Mary took Lilibet—for Margaret Rose was still too young to look upon the pale visage of approaching death—upstairs to the King's apartments, and there the new claimant in the long line bent down to take her own farewell.

Four days later, when the news of his passing was broken to her, this time by her mother, she burst into an uncontrollable fit of weeping. Nothing was safe, if even a king could not live for ever. She was not conscious at that moment that she had now

The two sisters win a cup at the Windsor Horse Show

spring, Lilibet could not help noticing a change in the grown-up's atmosphere. It was not simply that everyone was still in mourning for King George V. It was something else, something mysterious.

All through the summer and autumn, despite the happiness of learning to swim at the Bath Club, and such treats as visiting the *Queen Mary* in Southampton Docks, this feeling of tension increased. Conversations would break off suddenly, newspapers be tidied away in the schoolroom before she was allowed even to look at the pictures, until finally there came that Sunday when Uncle David arrived from Fort Belvedere to tea at Royal Lodge, and her mother sent Lilibet, with her younger sister in her charge, out to play in the gardens. "Now you have tea in your own little house," their mother had said.

Always before she would have had tea with Uncle David, too. Then why not today? What was happening? Why, instead of being allowed to meet the lady who had got out of the car with her hand on Uncle David's arm, must she and Margaret be hurried by Crawfie into the gardens to play at having their own tea party in The Little House—Y Bwthyn Bach—that the Welsh people had given them.

Of course, they loved it dearly. What little girls wouldn't? For it was complete in every detail, even to the miniature pictures on the drawing-room wall. As for the kitchen, they could cook in it, and wash up in it, and play at being grown-up to their hearts' content. But today, somehow, all their previous pleasure faded. At least, for Lilibet it did. She was curious, and for some reason she could not yet fathom, apprehensive. . . .

become second heir to the throne herself, only that she had lost for ever someone whom she dearly loved.

Before that same year was to draw to a close, she was to lose someone else, equally dear to her, but this time not in death: instead, to a life outside the golden railings that enclose the royal circle from the rest of the world.

Now that he was King, though not yet crowned, her Uncle David's informal visits to their own kingdom under the glass dome at the top of No. 145 Piccadilly grew less frequent, and then stopped altogether. Although she was only ten years old that

PREPARATION
FOR VICTORY

The balcony at Buckingham Palace. May 8th, 1945

Soon they were to break the news to her. Uncle David was going away for a long time, perhaps for ever, and they themselves were going to live in Buckingham Palace, instead. "What *for always?*" Lilibet looked at Crawfie in horror. For that would mean leaving her team of racing horses which filled the circular playing space under the dome.

Peeping over the banister rail far below they saw their father leaving for the Proclamation of his Accession on December 12th, 1936. He was suitably accoutred as an admiral of the fleet, and when he returned to lunch he would be King. What's more, you will have to curtsy to him every day of his life, their governess explained.

So they spent that morning, not learning the three R's, but practising their curtsies, and when their father reappeared they greeted him in the hall with a deep obeisance. He was surprised and touched, but he did not try to stop them. How could he?

For he knew, as his elder daughter was to know increasingly herself, that a new reign, a new phase in their joint destiny, had now inexorably begun. . . .

The first Armistice Day of the new Peace

CHAPTER THREE

"IF I am ever queen," Princess Elizabeth is quoted as saying when she was still a small girl, "I shall make a law that there must be no riding on Sundays. Horses should have a rest, too." However, once the abdication of the Duke of Windsor had become a constitutional reality, there was to be little more rest in the turbulent years ahead for her parents, whom Lilibet loved even more dearly than her unique collection of painted, wooden horses.

These had now been transported in a furniture van from their grazing ground under the dome of 145 Piccadilly, to line instead the red-carpeted corridor outside the row of apartments on the second floor of Buckingham Palace which early in 1937 became the new home of the two sisters and their two guardians, Alah and Crawfie. And the painted horses were still there on the morning of Lilibet's wedding day.

Of course, that great occasion when Westminster Abbey was to be filled with a glittering concourse of guests was still ten years away in the future. At the moment all the excitement was centred round the ceremony of King George VI's Coronation, and there was much friendly rivalry between his two daughters as to the length of the trains they would wear with their white dresses on the great day.

Margaret Rose, then aged six, was determined to be dressed exactly like her elder sister and proceeded to stage a sit-down strike when she was thwarted, giving a display of temperament which more than made up for her lack of inches.

"In the end I got my train, but, of course, it was *that much* shorter," Princess Margaret told me not long ago with a philosophical note in her voice as much as to say: it always is and always will be. On the occasion of this charmingly candid admission we were sitting at the desk of her apartment in the Palace which looks out over the courtyard, straight down the Mall towards Admiralty Arch, and the Princess was, most graciously, looking through the galley proofs of her biography that was soon to be published under my name.

Here and there she had pencilled her comments in the margin, and one of them concerned the length of her blue velvet train at the Coronation. She had been a little pudding of a girl then, wearing a special lightweight coronet and holding on to her aunt's hand throughout the enormous, terrifying journey up the whole length of the great nave, and now she was grown-up, a most elegant figure in her grey tie silk dress, but she had not forgotten a single incident of all that had happened on that historic May day.

Especially how, when later the Royal party came out on to the balcony to acknowledge the people's homage, Lilibet could see so much more easily over the top than she could!

For my own part, my most vivid memory of the service in the Abbey was of that moment when the newly crowned monarch and his consort had passed forth through the west door into the sunshine to greet the vast cheering throngs beyond, and the Queen Mother started slowly to make her own exit, a magnificent figure, all in gold. As she proceeded down the nave, suddenly, like corn in the wind, all the peeresses curtsied low before her as she passed, in spontaneous homage and in gratitude for the example she herself had set across the years of her sovereignty.

And what of the two small figures who followed, walking on either side of their aunt, the Princess Royal? Truthfully, from my own vantage point, high up in the transept, I could not differentiate between the length of their trains, but had I also been a fly upon one of the palace ceilings, I should have heard the elder of the two by over four years, remark grandly to her governess on their return from Westminster: "Oh, yes, Margaret was very good. I only had to nudge her once or twice when she played with her prayer books too loudly."

Lilibet might also admonish her younger sister in lordly terms not to hurry so obviously down the avenue between the guests towards the tea tent, when later that summer the first garden parties were held under the new régime. All the same she was still childish enough to upset a silver inkpot all over her head one morning because she was suddenly bored with her French lessons, and to fall into the lake and emerge covered from top to toe with green slime, in her efforts to find a duck's nest, *and* to make use of Margaret Rose's inborn genius for mimicry

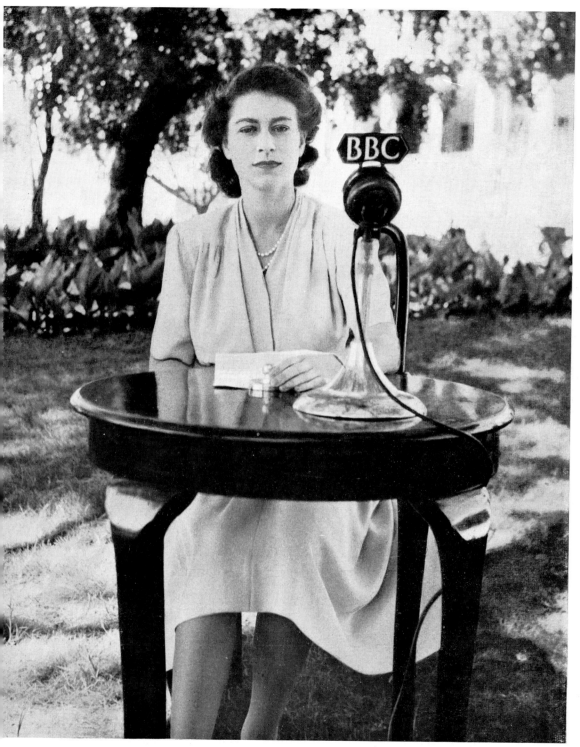

*On her twenty-first birthday our future Queen speaks from her heart
to the youth of the whole Empire*

SOUTH AFRICAN TOUR 1947

Father and daughter look into the future together

in a manner that nearly caused corporal punishment as its sequel.

What happened on that occasion still produces a reminiscent chuckle today from the Court official concerned. They had only been a few months in their new London home, which needs no less than forty Mrs. Mopps to clean it, possesses its own post office, fire and police stations, and where one man does nothing else but wind up the collection of two hundred and fifty clocks first started by George III. So it was not surprising that the two children decided that something must be done to enliven the tradition-haunted atmosphere. Whereupon they got busy on the newly installed nursery telephone.

The result was that three times in the same morning, one of the King's secretaries presented himself at the door of his royal master's study. "You sent for me, Your Majesty?" The King looked up from the pile of official papers he was studying and shook his head, puzzled, until suddenly a great light dawned. "I'll deal with this myself," he said, ringing his bell. This time he did want to see someone, and on very important business indeed.

Soon a way, and a most sensible way, was found of harnessing their animal high spirits. Now, in that precious hour after tea, a series of black boxes full of State documents formed an impregnable barrier between their father and the pillow fights and games of hide and seek they were accustomed to have every evening. And the acres of passages at the palace would have been so perfect, too! However, instead, they formed their own Girl Guide group, from the daughters of officials and staff, inside the Palace.

The original idea came from Crawfie, a most excellent one which was enthusiastically endorsed by her employers at once. Nevertheless, when they sought to enlist the aid of Miss Violet Synge, later to be Guide Commissioner for the whole country, she was at first doubtful as to how the project could hope to succeed.

"The whole point about the Guide Movement," this high-up officer explained, "is that all Guides must look upon each other as sisters."

But that, of course, was exactly what the princesses were longing to do. Inevitably they were isolated from the companionship of schoolgirls of their own age. In the days when they had played in the gardens off Hamilton Place they had seen other children with their nannies in the park, but always in the distance,.

Now it would be different. Lilibet refused to be defeated, even when it was pointed out that her sister was too young to be a proper Guide. "Oh, but Miss Synge," she protested. "Margaret loves getting dirty, don't you? and she would love to have a chance to cook sausages on sticks. And she has very strong legs. Show Miss Synge your legs, Margaret."

In the end a compromise was effected, Margaret became a Brownie and with a companion of her own was attached to the senior troop. Their father made only one proviso. He abominated those long black stockings, then part of the uniform. So the Palace troop wore knee-length beige stockings instead, and what started as a private innovation was later to be adopted by the Movement as correct dress all over the world. Which means that a new generation of Guides have a special debt of gratitude for the aesthetic good sense of Lilibet's father.

It was for him a proud moment when the daughter, who right from the early years he had sensed was so much part of himself, appeared in public for the first time in uniform—a uniform that she had truly earned the right to wear.

This was on June 19th, 1938, when in the quadrangle of Windsor Castle, Princess Elizabeth stood beside her parents, Queen Mary and the Princess Royal, while a thousand Girl Guides, representing all parts of the Empire, marched past on their way to attend a special service in St. George's Chapel. And as her fellow-guides obeyed the order, "Eyes Right", they all saw on the butcher-blue cotton tunic, for which Lilibet had been personally measured at the headquarters in Buckingham Palace Road, a white strip to show that its wearer was now second in command of her own patrol.

That year, too, Princess Elizabeth accepted her first public appointment. She became President of the Children's League of the Princess Elizabeth of York Hospital at Shadwell. And that year also she accompanied her parents to the launching ceremony of the Cunard liner number 552, a ship that was destined to cover itself with glory, both in war and peace.

Yes, it was the *Queen Elizabeth* and at the launching, gazing up at the great sides of the ship, the Princess clutched her mother's arm in her excitement and exclaimed: "But, Mummy, there isn't room for it. The river isn't wide enough."

Whereupon the Queen laughed as she turned to Lord Aberconway, chairman of John Brown's shipyards at Clydebank, and replied for him with the pride of a good

Scotswoman: "You will see what they can do on the Clyde."

Now Lilibet was twelve years old, tall for her age and slender, with her mother's beautiful colouring, but a deep look of her father in her eyes and her sweet, rather shy smile. Now Princess Elizabeth was accepted as heir presumptive, and the Cabinet held a meeting to determine what steps should be taken for the Princess's education in all the intricate, specialized knowledge that must be hers if she was to be fitted unfalteringly for the role that she would one day have to play in her country's affairs.

"Constitutional History" was the first and the most important subject to be added to her schoolroom curriculum and for its elucidation the assistance was sought of the then Vice-Provost of Eton, Sir Henry Marten, who every week gave his royal pupil private tuition in his own book-lined study. He also gave her a reading list and questioned her afterwards as to her own reactions to the works of Professor Trevelyan, whose *English Social History* has already become a classic, and Lord Elton's brilliant treatise, *Imperial Commonwealth*.

Later, the elderly scholar and the young girl on the threshold of great events, of history in the making, were to have weekly discussions on current affairs. She was a serious and conscientious student, always asking questions, always wanting to know why, and always grateful for the calm, considered wisdom of her tutor who, in one way, was as young as she was. He loved sweet things and in the war, when sweet things were hard to come by, in gratitude for all she had learnt, his pupil would send him parcels of honey that had been presents to her family from overseas.

Even if it had not been rationed Lilibet could not have bought the honey herself for her pocket money up to the age of fourteen was only a shilling a week and when she went to Sunday service in the chapel at Windsor with her parents, the King would surreptitiously pass a shilling over to her for the offertory and another for her sister, while he and the Queen would each give a pound note.

Parliament might vote the heir presumptive to the throne an allowance of six thousand pounds a year, but the money had no more reality for her yet than the expeditions that she made under her grandmother's guidance to the Royal Mint, where she saw her father's new seal being created, and to the Bank of England.

On this occasion they were honoured by the presence of that legendary figure Montagu Norman, and there in the vaults were the piles and piles of gold bricks. For the bullion really looked like ordinary bricks and the princesses were secretly rather disappointed. They had expected something more glamorous, much more like the transformation scene of a pantomime than this. However, their host assured them that it really was gold and they were very welcome to any of it, as a souvenir, that they could carry away with them. They tried very hard, but it was no use. . . .

They also tried very hard that spring to do what they were told when they had to put on their gas masks and pretend to take refuge in an air raid shelter newly constructed out of a dungeon at Windsor Castle, with seven-foot thick walls. They felt safe enough there, but was it only pretending?

That was the question which everyone was asking themselves as the summer of 1939 drew on. The King and Queen might fulfil their Canadian and American tour, smiling, smiling as though they hadn't a care in the world, and be reunited with their children on board the *Empress of Britain* in Portsmouth Harbour. The loving gaiety of that day might make it seem as though such beautiful liners could only be used for peace-time cruises and missions of goodwill, never as a troopship in a submarine-infested sea. . . .

But August came and even inside the palace the growing weight of anxiety could no longer be kept from the children of the house. Their mother seemed suddenly very tired, their father very silent, until at last Margaret piped up: "Who is this horrid old Hitler who is being such a nuisance and spoiling everything?"

The answer was to evacuate the princesses to Scotland and keep them there at Birkhall (the small house near Balmoral where later the Duke and Duchess of Edinburgh were to spend part of their honeymoon), until right up to Christmas, as far away as possible from blacked-out London.

They spent their time knitting (rather badly) and passing round tea at the village sewing parties and going for rides over the moors on their ponies, so when it was announced over the wireless that the sirens had been sounded in London, their governess tried to explain to them what that meant. But the peace which surrounded them was still absolute and the war only became a reality, at least for the elder sister, the day that the radio had to admit that one of Britain's finest ships, *The Royal Oak*, had been sunk.

Lilibet jumped out of her chair by the fire in her distress. "Oh, Crawfie," she exclaimed, "all those brave sailors."

She was still worrying, because she was so much more serious-minded than her sister, so very grown-up for her age, when the children were reunited with their parents at Sandringham at Christmas, and Lilibet wrote to her governess on holiday in her own home: "I kept thinking of those sailors, Crawfie, and what Christmas must be like in their homes."

She was her father's daughter, and this was his Service. And then, too, perhaps, she was remembering the visit that summer which all the family had paid to Dartmouth College, and the cadet, with the look of the young Viking, who, like so many others of the ranks that her father had inspected, would soon be having his own baptism at sea.

But this particular youth stood out henceforth in her memory. Not because, like herself, he was of royal blood, but because he had been so gay and amusing the whole week-end. Prince Philip of Greece had jumped the tennis net backwards and forwards to show how much higher he could jump than any girl, and teased Margaret unmercifully for being a plump pudding, and stuffed himself enormously on board the royal yacht, sympathetically encouraged by his host who reminded his daughters that this would be their guest's last meal of the day.

And all the time Lilibet watched him in fascinated silence. Apart from her cousins, the Lascelles boys (and because they were cousins, they didn't really count) he was the first boy that she had ever come into intimate contact with who didn't treat her as someone very important and apart, but instead as

Now the whole world knew of their betrothal—
July 10th, 1947

something slightly inferior, just because she was a girl.

She was enchanted with his brashness, and when the time came for the yacht to weigh anchor and many of the cadets followed its progress into the Channel, in whatever craft they could muster, Lilibet was thrilled because it was the fair young Viking who hung on longest to the chase. Borrowing her father's binoculars, she watched him excitedly until he, finally, was lost to sight.

However, not from her life. For during the war years, whenever he came on leave, staying with his relations the Mountbattens, Philip would pay a flying visit to Windsor Castle, where, as a full-fledged matelot, he would change the atmosphere instantly with his exuberant high spirits, his intense masculinity, his complete lack of standing on ceremony.

On one occasion he and David Milford-Haven, later to be his best man at his wedding, rolled back the carpets three nights running and took the two sisters for their partners, treating them as though they were grown-up, exquisite young ladies of fashion in a London ballroom, instead of two schoolgirls incarcerated for the duration of the war in an ancient and somewhat moribund castle.

Still, it was the safest place for them. Early in 1940 their parents had decided to move them there from Scotland and they had stayed on, right through the blitzes and, later, the flying bomb period. When the raids were at their very worst it was suggested by some members of the Government that the princesses should be sent to safety in Canada. But their mother would not hear of it. "I would not let them go without

me," was her emphatic reply, "and I could never leave the King."

Her answer was typical of someone who is admired throughout the Empire as much for the way that she has fulfilled the role of wife and mother as of queen during a war-scarred reign. And it was typical of her, too, that one week-end at Windsor, coming down to dinner late, she should say in explanation, "I have just been talking things out with Lilibet."

A revealing phrase that lights up their whole relationship. That particular night the mother and daughter had been "talking out" the indiscriminate bombing of the children's school at Lewisham which had just happened and was to shock every home in the land. When later the Queen went to visit in hospital the maimed victims—Cecil Beaton made a picture of one of them which haunts me still—she took with her a huge bunch of bananas that Lord Louis Mountbatten had brought the princesses from North Africa.

Of course they wanted to do so much more, and there was so little that they could do yet. It was imperative that they should be kept safe and hidden. So they had to be content, for the present, in joining the Sea Rangers, and getting up pantomimes to swell the Wool Fund in the castle, and continuing their lessons, though Princess Margaret refused point blank to study her German verbs.

It was her elder sister who was the conscientious one. Margaret was adept from a very early age in finding excuses for not doing what she did not want to do. And on this occasion, Hitler provided the perfect excuse! All the same, when I suggested on one occasion, years later, that she and her sister must have been awfully bored shut away from life for five whole years, the Princess shook her head most emphatically.

"Windsor Castle may have seemed like a gloomy prison to our governess in the war because she would be alone in the evenings, and have to find her way down draughty passages, badly lit, to dinner when we were warmly tucked up in bed. But Lilibet and I love Windsor the best of all our homes. It has such atmosphere."

Anyone who has ever looked up the Broad Walk towards the castle on a summer's day, or again, said farewell to this symbol of England's greatness when its turrets are silhouetted against a scarlet evening sky, will appreciate exactly what the Princess was trying to convey to me.

For my own part, I had a memorable visit to the castle myself towards the end of the war when I was one of the privileged guests at the last of the pantomimes devised by Princess Elizabeth, Princess Margaret, and their dear friend, the local schoolmaster, Hubert Tannar.

There was certainly nothing gloomy or prison-like about the atmosphere of the Waterloo Chamber that afternoon. On the contrary it was an hilarious occasion when the laughter was led by the King and Queen seated just in front of me who, I noticed, applauded most loudly when the "leading lady" of *Old Mother Red Riding Boots* decided to appear for one of her numbers in a late Victorian bathing-dress, looking suddenly very much like her grandmother, Queen Mary.

I don't know whether the cast or the audience enjoyed themselves more. Anyway, one had a feeling that the two leading actresses were saying to themselves: we shall never have such a chance to let ourselves go again.

But they did have one more chance. On VE-night, their parents allowed them, suitably escorted by some of the young Guards officers who had been stationed at Windsor guarding the castle, to slip out of a side entrance to Buckingham Palace and mingle with the rejoicing, peace-delirious crowds.

It is true that Princess Elizabeth had already enjoyed a faint measure of freedom when she had enrolled in the A.T.S. and, having taken a complete course in car maintenance, had had the adventure of driving a superior officer right through the traffic of London. But now, instead, she was completely off duty, a pedestrian, anonymous, incognito, seeing the world and life outside the palace gates from a very different angle than ever before—or ever after. Indeed, one of her escorts that night has told me how they were jostled and caught in the scrambling, tight-packed throng, but for once the Princess didn't care or feel responsible when her younger sister gaily knocked off a hat here and there.

As for her own safety that evening, had she been asked what her feelings were, there is little doubt she would have replied, as she did two years later when it was suggested by a close friend that she must have felt very nervous on her wedding day, playing her part in all the complicated arrangements inside and outside the Abbey.

"No, I didn't feel at all afraid," the Princess replied, "because I knew in my heart that so many people were wishing me well."

But that, of course, belongs to the next chapter in our story.

44

The Great Day itself November 20th, 1947

In the Abbey

On the balcony at Buckingham Palace

Husband and Wife

CHAPTER FOUR

"I DO hope now that she has to go out and perform public duties they will let her do young things as long as possible. Not too many hospitals at first. Now the Presidency of the College of Music was perfect. She adores music, and at the next table at tea afterwards, the students who received their medals from her were such a happy group. Why, they were all laughing loudly."

Buckingham Palace seemed very silent and still, as with these words of the Queen's lady-in-waiting sounding in my ears, I made my way down the scarlet-carpeted stairs from the King's sitting-room on the first floor. It was war time then, and all the marble plinths in the corridors had been beheaded of their busts for the duration. Very naked and bare they looked, I remember, and at the foot of each one, as a precaution against further emergencies, rested a sandbag.

Certainly no one could describe any members of our Royal Family as figures of sand, I also remember thinking that afternoon. At the same moment it occurred to me how it would be down these same stairs the King and Queen had walked, without undue haste, when the bomb had fallen outside in the courtyard and smashed in the windows of their own personal sitting-room.

Of course, the glass had long since been replaced, in many other windows besides, and time has swallowed up a multitude of memories of those days, but, for my own part, I confess I find it difficult to forget the nondescript pieces of cardboard blocking up the gaps in the windows, just as I can still hear quite clearly in my ears those sudden, heartfelt words of my hostess that afternoon.

Her words came from the heart because she had spent a lifetime of service, following always a few steps behind her Royal mistress, the discreet shadow who equally must never feel tired or bored. While the reason for my own presence in the Palace that day—in contrast such an exciting novelty for me— was that I had been commissioned to write a profile of Princess Elizabeth for her official coming of age, on her eighteenth birthday.

But another whole year was to pass before, the war over at last, the subject of my portrait was free to come back to London and move once more into her old apartments in the Palace. Her bedroom was still her favourite shade of pink, with chintz covers for the chairs, and though they gave her a sitting-room of her own, she still had breakfast every morning in the old nursery with Margaret. Their childhood string of horses were still on the landing, almost as though the last six years had never happened.

But they had. She had disappeared from public gaze, a pretty child with a mop of fair curls, Lilibet: she had returned, a graceful well-built young woman, weighing nine stone eleven, with a touch of lipstick and her wavy hair neatly arranged now to fit the line of her head, Elizabeth. Lilibet and Elizabeth. There was a considerable difference to be recognized more and more in every public engagement that the Princess carried out on her own.

Of course, these no longer needed to be, for security's sake, performed almost in secret like that inspection of a Guards' battalion, as their colonel-in-chief, to which I have already referred in an earlier chapter. Instead her diary began to be filled up months and months in advance—that Re-

membrance Day of 1945, the first to be observed for six years, Princess Elizabeth, dressed in the A.T.S. uniform of a junior commander placed her own wreath upon the Cenotaph—and altogether, it was a heavier and heavier list, but one which quite truthfully the heir presumptive welcomed.

And for two reasons. First because she had inherited from her father an already deeply developed sense of duty, and secondly, because the sum total of all these appearances in public gave her many, varying glimpses of the people, over whom one day she was destined to rule.

NOW THE UNCEASING ROUND OF PUBLIC LIFE BEGINS

49   *Lord Nuffield welcomes a very special visitor*

Anna, the daughter of two distinguished artists of the theatre, Raymond Massey and Adrianne Allen, presents a bouquet to the greatest star of all

*These Italia Conti
dancing pupils will
remember this afternoon
all their lives*

It must be remembered that, through no fault of her own, up till then such appearances had been very limited. All through the war years as soon as dusk approached, the King's advisers insisted on both Lilibet and Margaret being safely within the thick stone walls of Windsor Castle. Never, under any circumstances, must they be permitted to spend a night in the Metropolis.

Sometimes, of course, they might make a trip to London for lunch, and have the thrilling experience of sitting next to Mr. Churchill, who, with a twinkle in his eye, would expansively and confidentially tell them all the latest "inside news" which they would only realize afterwards they had already seen, couched in rather different language, in that morning's papers! But more often their presence there wasn't a holiday from lessons at all, but simply an appointment with the dentist that had brought them to Town.

But never an appointment for shopping or trying on clothes. Because, like other children, they had to "make do" with their coupons: Margaret with her elder sister's clothes, Lilibet with no real party dresses, except one or two of her mother's pre-war ball gowns, with their dateless crinoline skirts, simplified and altered by the Royal dressmaker, Norman Hartnell.

But now it was all going to be different. Peace was here, and Elizabeth was nineteen, an intoxicating age for any girl, with a great deal of leeway to make up, in her case, where her personal life was concerned. All through the war she hadn't been able to see one West End play, or one single London concert she loved so much, but, instead, all her good music had come to her over the radio, which became, in consequence, her most constant companion. For the lighter side, she and her sister would never miss their weekly date with Tommy Handley, in *Itma*. On the other hand, except for the relays of Guards officers, on duty at Windsor, who would be invited in turn to lunch with the Princesses, she had scarcely met any young men of her own generation.

Of course, had it not been for hostilities, her father would have given her a wonderful coming-out ball. Instead, she missed all the fun of those teenage years which other girls have had before and since the war. For Elizabeth those years had scarcely existed, and certainly could never now be recaptured, in peace time.

It was quite different for Margaret. She was only about to be fifteen when VJ-Day finally dawned and the King voiced the whole Empire's thankfulness in a broadcast from his study at Buckingham Palace, and St. James' Park was suddenly transformed into a fairyland of floodlighting. Margaret had missed nothing really, it was all ahead of her, and though her elder sister didn't allow herself any futile regrets, remembering all the bombed-out victims, it was not surprising that she should seem rather serious and grown-up for her age.

And it must be realized, too, that even when the blackout blinds were up at last, and it was safe once more for the Princess to move about freely, day or night, that still didn't mean that she could go out alone with any young man, like other girls in her social circle. Instead, there must always be a party of four, even to a theatre, and preferably six or eight. That was a strict protocol, never to be broken or disregarded.

A year or so later, the King might give his daughter, for her twenty-first birthday, her own car, with its distinctive number plate of H.R.H. 1, but she could never drive it anywhere without a bodyguard in the back, or a detective in another car following at a discreet distance, and never, never, must she allow one of her escorts at a private dance to take her home himself.

One privilege alone, as regards her private and personal life was left to her. She could, by Royal custom, following her mother's example, open her own letters every morning, before her lady-in-waiting or her own secretary saw them. Yes, now she had her own lady-in-waiting, and soon a male secretary to cope with the flood of charity appeals, as well as her own standard, crest and coat-of-arms—and, surely, most important

*Princess Elizabeth receives the Freedom
of the City of London at the Guildhall*

The Colonel of the Regiment inspects the Grenadier Guards at Chelsea Barracks

"Can I have my finger back, please?" the visitor said

of all in her secret heart, her own follower.

For, because of the rigid rules of court etiquette, apart altogether from the question marks inevitably raised at the appearance at the Palace gate. of a Royal suitor, that charming, old-fashioned word "follower" exactly describes the standing of Lieutenant Philip Mountbatten at this moment when he would follow the announcements of the Royal Family's future movements and hope, with a little manœuvring and a little briefing from the inside, to make his well-earned spots of leave synchronize with invitations for some of the same parties.

It wasn't easy, but then the course of true love seldom is. He could not turn up at the Palace without a personal invitation from the Princess's parents. Or if Elizabeth asked him herself to have a glass of sherry before dinner in her own apartments there always had to be a chaperone in the room. Even if it was only Margaret, she was there, and passing through that adolescent stage that all girls go through when she wanted to show how grown-up she was herself, and demanded just as much attention from Philip as though he were her own admirer.

Then, even when they got invited to the same private parties, or went to supper at the Savoy or Ciro's, the most they could hope for would be a couple of dances during the evening. Had there been more, had they seemed too obviously to enjoy each other's company, people would have started talking, or rather, they would have some definite evidence at last.

Of what? Why, that the young sailor with the very blond hair and the very blue eyes, who had been mentioned in dispatches for his part in the Battle of Matapan, and for whom Lilibet had wrapped up parcels and saved her chocolate ration, now occupied more than a sisterly place in the affections of Elizabeth: in truth he owned every bit of her heart that was not already given to her family, or to her future, in the direct line of accession to the throne.

She could not tell anyone in so many words, least of all her follower. She did not really know herself how the transition had happened but that spring and early summer of 1946 the very air smelt differently and she would find herself playing over and over again a certain record from the pile that stood beside the radiogram in her sitting-room at Buckingham Palace.

It was a song from the score of *Oklahoma!* which recently had been sent to her as a present in an album from America. In the war, she and her sister used to sing the re-frain for months on end of "This is the Army, Mr. Jones", but now her favourite was something very new and very different, and she sang to herself with the picture of Philip, in a naval uniform, wearing a beard, on the table beside her bed. And the song? "People Will Say We're in Love".

Then one day the bubble of happiness momentarily burst. Or rather, the bubble of belief that if you are a Royal princess, heir to a great inheritance, you can keep anything as private and precious as your first and last love affair to yourself, for long. It could not be, but the way that the truth was brought home to Elizabeth hurt her terribly, for the moment.

The King's daughter had been touring a factory, one of the endless entries in her diary of duty, and as she came to the top of a line of cheering operatives, very clearly above the roar, a voice could be heard shouting, "Where's Philip?" It took all her royal training in control not to turn her head, not to betray her acute embarrassment.

The truth was her shyness had not lessened with the years, and shut away within an inevitably narrow circle, she had no consciousness of how strong were the growing rumours up and down the country. Until the shock of this moment. And now it was difficult at first to realize that this good-natured sally was only a vociferous part of the immense affection that the people, whom she longed to serve, in their turn felt towards her. All the world loves a romance and all the world wanted her to be happy, because it is not easy to deceive public opinion, and public opinion believed that she was as nice a girl as you could hope to find in any home.

So everyone waited now expectantly for an official announcement to come from her father. But it did not come. Philip went to stay at Balmoral, for the whole length of his Foreign Service leave, that autumn, but still no definite news of any engagement. On the contrary. The announcement, when it did happen, was something quite different. *Both* Princesses would be accompanying their parents on their four-month sea trip in the *Vanguard* and tour of South Africa early in the New Year. And there was no mention of Philip being in the party. . . .

There was no mention of him for the very good reason that Elizabeth's parents wanted

Princess Elizabeth becomes Lady of the Order of the Garter, and her husband is created Knight Companion at Windsor Chapel

Two designs from the Queen's wardrobe created by her dressmaker
Mr. Norman Hartnell

Norman Hartnell.

The Passing-out Parade at the Royal Air Force College, Cranwell

to see what effect the long absence would have on the romance. It was to be a testing period of reflection, while everyone could finally make up their minds, the King as well as the daughter who one day would have to sit upon the same throne and bear the same burdens of office.

And what man should be at her side in the tortuous years ahead? Did it matter that her suitor, who looked so utterly English had, in fact, an overwhelming amount of foreign blood in his veins? Would Philip be prepared tactfully to play his part in the same minor key as the Good Albert? Or would he, being a sailor and used to giving commands on the quarter-deck, find it intolerably difficult always to walk a few steps behind his wife?

There were many doubts in Court circles, many question marks. They can be admitted frankly now that the sequel has turned out such a constitutional success. Just as it can be stated with equal frankness that never for a moment were there any doubts in the Princess's own mind, never once did she waver throughout her long separation—

and four months can seem an eternity if you are in love—when during the time that the Royal party spent on South African soil, they travelled eight thousand miles alone.

All the receptions, the handshakings, the addresses of welcome, the train journeys, the visiting of famous beauty spots and historic monuments, such as the day that they climbed right up to "World's View", the burial place of Cecil Rhodes, and Elizabeth did the last quarter of a mile of the grass in her stockinged feet because the heel of one of the Queen's own shoes had come off . . . all, all must have seemed like a giant soporific for her, in one way, so unreal against the urgent beating of her heart.

And yet, in another way, her heart was just as much in her job as ever, as she proved when it came to her twenty-first birthday. Other girls would be free to enjoy themselves, as they wished on such a day, they could belong to themselves, with the key of the door in their hands. How different it was for the Princess!

Certainly she was showered with gifts of jewels, both from South Africa and from the vault of her own family heirlooms, including, from her parents, a most beautiful ruby and diamond necklace that I was to see her wearing years later at the Mountbatten party at Broadlands I have already described.

strain upon the King who had lost over a stone in weight, and was never to recapture entirely again his former resilience. The toll on his health that was to lead first to the operation on his leg and later to the second, more serious one on his chest, had inexorably begun.

But for the Princesses the homeward journey was a delightful interlude, when they indulged in treasure hunts with the snotties, while their parents rested before the demands of another season's panoply just ahead.

And when the *Vanguard* finally docked and the Duke of Gloucester came on board to greet his brother, it was plainly noticeable that Princess Elizabeth was in a particularly happy mood. Indeed, she made no effort to conceal her delight at her journey's end and now and again executed a few dance steps on the quarter-deck as though she could hear an invisible band playing her favourite tune.

She had promised her parents that she would be patient so as to make certain that

*Another day,
she drives in state
through the heart
of her capital*

she felt the same about her follower on her return, but anyone who saw her smiling face that day could have no doubts that her transparent joy did not spring solely from being on her own native soil again.

All the same, the Princess and her suitor had to wait almost another two months before their betrothal was formally proclaimed in the Court Circular, and even on the evening before, when the official news at last from the Palace was being sped by wire and telephone all over the world,

the young couple could not be together. He was on duty down at the naval station at Corsham, she was a guest at a private dance for the coming-out of one of her friends, Miss Fay James.

I was at the dance myself, though when I accepted the invitation of my hostess, Lady Serena James, who had been a close friend for many years, and in whose Yorkshire home I recuperated when I came back from the wars, I had no idea that the guests would all inevitably feel they

The boys of Cheltenham College take their own snapshots of their future monarch

were taking part in an historic occasion.

Instead, I just imagined that it would be the traditional kind of coming-out party that the Princess herself had missed, through the war, set, in this case, against the magnificence of Apsley House, where at Hyde Park Corner successive Dukes of Wellington had lived since a grateful nation presented the property to the victor of the Battle of Waterloo.

And now this was the last time that a private ball would ever be held there.

A visit to the Circus at Olympia

Henceforth the custodianship of the treasures would pass back to the nation, and as we danced that night by the light of thousands of candles, we gradually became conscious that the magic and beauty and the excitement of the evening belonged to something that was already like a legend, so that one day when we were old ourselves we would talk of this ball even as our great-grandparents had talked of that other one, held in Brussels on the eve of the battle.

This battle, such as it was, was resolved at last, and there was victory for the girl in the exquisite taffeta crinoline, with a corsage of gold sequins that matched her sandals. She wore two ropes of pearls, and the tiny diamond wrist-watch that had been her father's present long ago, and no ring yet upon the third finger of her left hand. Nevertheless, there was an unmistakable air of overflowing happiness as she danced every dance till midnight came and, across the park, Big Ben struck with its solemn intonation. It was a new day; her day at last.

Two hours later, when I left myself, the Princess was still at the dance, though very early the next morning an excited girl burst into her governess's room, at last waving something on her finger. It was her engagement ring of diamonds, and though it was much too large, and had to go back to the jeweller's to be refitted, what did that matter? "I wanted you to be the first to see it, and to congratulate me, Crawfie."

While at the same moment at breakfast tables throughout the country, with warm feelings of congratulation towards the Princess who one day would be their Queen and whom they had already grown to love like someone in their own family, Elizabeth's

countrymen and women read the formal proclamation:

" It is with the greatest pleasure that the King and Queen announce the betrothal of their dearly beloved daughter the Princess Elizabeth to Lieutenant Philip Mountbatten, R.N., son of the late Prince Andrew of Greece and the Princess Alice of Battenburg, to which union the King has gladly given his consent.

That happy day was July 10th, 1947. . . .

CHAPTER FIVE

THE morning of November the 20th, 1947, dawned grey and chilly with more than a hint of rain in the low clouds on the horizon which mercifully, was to hold off, except for a slight drizzle, throughout the day. But inside Buckingham Palace on the breakfast tray of the Princess upon whom the eyes of the whole world were turned at that moment, was a welcome touch of brightness; a bunch of white carnations from the bridegroom.

With these in her hands, the girl of twenty-one so soon to be the Duchess of Edinburgh, crossed to the windows of her bedroom and, still in her dressing-gown, looked out down the Mall at the vast concourse of people who had collected there during the night. In her heart at that moment must have been a strange mingling of pride and humility that her wedding day should mean so much to so many.

Perhaps she was thinking, too, of all the thousands of wedding presents that had been sent to her, during those hectic four months of preparation since the announcement of her engagement, from well-wishers throughout the Empire. These had included bundles of clothing coupons, more precious, in a way, than the piece of Welsh-quarried gold, presented by the people of Wales, that had gone to the making of her wedding ring.

"But there's enough for *two* rings," the delighted girl, whose engagement hoop of diamonds, now fitted, had exclaimed. "We can save a piece for Margaret."

The coupons, of course, all had to be sent back since it was against the law of the land to accept them. Moreover, up till that time, it had also been against Royal precedent to accept any wedding presents except from personal friends or public bodies. On this occasion, however, the Palace officials relented at the express wish of the bride's mother who felt that so much affection had gone to the giving it would be a cruel thing to spoil the pleasure of the donors and their share in this happy day.

Nevertheless, some of the presents were on the strange side. Not the dozens of pairs of nylons—they were wonderful!—but one parcel when it was unwrapped contained two very soggy, burnt pieces of toast which two young women had been making at the moment when they heard the news of the engagement announced over the radio. Another parcel, done up in many layers of brown paper, weighed so heavily that for a moment it was thought it *might* be a bomb. Instead it turned out to be a small piece of Mount Snowdon sent by a very old man for luck.

Luck! As the bride of a few hours ahead stood there at the windows of her apartment in the Palace, surely it must have been in her mind, too, how very lucky she was, not so much to have been born to be Queen of England one day as to be marrying now the man of her choice, utterly her own choice, and not some princeling chosen in mediaeval times by cynical counsellors round the throne, plotting their own aggrandisement.

Now there was a knock on the door and her devoted maid and friend, whom her mistress affectionately calls Bo-Bo, appeared, reminding her that her moment of communion, of belonging to herself, was over and that the time had come for her to be decked in the dress of ivory satin with its glittering train of embroidered net over which the world outside the Palace gates had been speculating, in a mounting fever, for weeks.

Was it really the most beautiful dress that any Royal bride had ever worn? It had certainly cost enough. For over seventeen hundred pounds was the actual cost of the materials and the embroidery and the working hours of the seamstresses that went to its making, and that not counting all the other hours given over to its fitting and, most important of all, the guarding of the secret.

Norman Hartnell, the family's dressmaker, then and now, had been harried almost out of his life by "pirates" seeking to snatch the details of the dress before the day and copy it for sale in America. His work girls had been waylaid at the corner of the street and offered a king's ransom if they would disclose what they knew. But, as always, they were too proud and too loyal.

In desperation someone even took premises overlooking one angle of the workrooms at the back in their efforts to get an authentic picture of what was going on inside. Indeed, it got to a pitch when the proprietor of that famous salon in Bruton Street with its elegant grey walls and glass chandeliers had to hire an armed guard at night to keep at bay unwelcome and unlawful intruders.

There had been other alarums and excursions, too. Half way through the making of the dress a rumour started—perhaps by a jealous rival—that Japanese silkworms were being used for the silk. Balmoral telephoned Bruton Street and an official announcement had to be made to state that, on the contrary, *Chinese* silkworms, now domiciled in Scotland—or should one write "naturalized"?—were solely being employed in the spinning. The actual domicile was Dunfermline, the home town of the Princess's beloved governess, Crawfie. What could be more suitable than that?

And then that morning of the wedding when everything seemed ready and perfect at last, and her parents and her bridesmaids and those of the Palace servants who,

*Grand National Day
at Aintree*

The Oaks at Epsom

The Royal Procession at Ascot

through duty, could not be in the Abbey, had been invited to the bride's apartments to see her clothed in all her glorious finery, even then the last of the crises that go with every wedding weren't yet quite resolved.

For suddenly no one could find the double row of pearls, one of her wedding presents from her father, that the Princess was determined to wear. And where, oh where, was the bridal bouquet?

At last it was suggested that the pearls might have been sent over to St. James' Palace with the rest of the wedding presents placed there on show, but when her secretary, Mr. John Coville, dashed across in a car to fetch them, the police on guard thought

his story very odd, and insisted on sending him back to the Palace, in charge of two sergeants to test his credentials! While, as for the bouquet, that finally came to light in a cupboard where an over-zealous footman had placed it, intending to keep it cool and fresh and out of the way of the general excitement.

Of course, in the Abbey none of the 2,000 guests knew anything of these mishaps. Instead, as they waited in a rising tension of expectation, all they could hear above the music of the organ playing Elgar's "Sonata in G Major" and Bach's "Jesu, Joy of Man's Desiring" was the rising crescendo of the horses' hooves in each of

SNAPSHOTS FROM HER MALTA ALBUM   *In the garden of the Villa Guardamangia, Malta*

When on holiday at Malta her public duties became a special pleasure

Saddle Club Dance at Malta

the processions as they drew near the West Door.

First there was the arrival of Queen Mary, dressed all in blue, and the cheers that greeted her, and then the bride's mother, magnificent in apricot, and finally the greatest outburst of all, heralding the safe arrival of the bride. A moment later, there was a thrilling fanfare of trumpets as up the nave, side by side with her father, she slowly came, pale but very lovely, with her veil thrown back, in the true tradition of Royal brides.

For those of us who were there in the Abbey or heard the ceremony relayed over the wireless, there were moments of that particular wedding service that will long linger in our memory, especially the firm clarity of the bride's voice when she promised both to honour and obey, and the beautiful singing of the psalm, "The Lord is My Shepherd", so familiar, and yet on this occasion, because it was set in harmony to a Scottish air, unfamiliar to those of us who dwell in the south. In consequence, it almost seemed as though one was hearing the words for the first time. Yet none the less moving for that.

Still, I shall always think myself that the most moving moment of all came at the very

end, after the Archbishop of Canterbury's blessing and the second fanfare of trumpets had blazed out before the singing of the National Anthem. Then, with the signing of the register, it was all over, just like other weddings.

No, not quite like other weddings. Because, although this had been a family event, it had been transacted in the bosom of history. So, at that last moment in the Abbey, before, hand in hand with her bridegroom dressed in the naval uniform that he had richly earned, the Princess passed once more down the vast, shimmering nave, spontaneously she curtsied both to Queen Mary and to the King of Britain. It was at once a gesture of loving devotion to her father, and of loyal devotion to her Sovereign and the Crown. A gesture long to be remembered by those who witnessed it.

How different was that other moment hours later, when, the wedding party over the young couple were about to leave in an open carriage for the first part of their honeymoon to be spent at Broadlands. Whereupon the bride's mother and father led the scramble across the courtyard of Buckingham Palace to wave and cheer them on their way.

The cheers lasted all along the route to Waterloo, and Elizabeth and Philip went on waving back, and smiling as the vocal demonstrations of goodwill towards them

Off-duty snapshots from her holiday scrapbook

and their merged future surrounded them, like a safety-curtain. They were very happy but very tired. And very human. For waiting on the platform for them was the bride's favourite Corgi, and into the carriage with them it jumped joyfully, no longer needed as a chaperone but taking its rightful place in their newly married state.

Broadlands, the Hampshire home of the Mountbattens, is, as I have already said, very beautiful in all weathers, and despite the grandeur of its pillared entrance and the richness of the silk hangings in the sitting-room that the honeymooners will have used on this occasion, it has a friendly, most welcoming air which I sometimes attribute myself, to the charm of the river running through its grounds.

Along the banks of the Test, during the next few days, they walked and rode, thankful for the respite and the intimate atmosphere of each other's company, really alone together, for the first time since they had met as boy and girl upon the banks of another river, the Dart. How much they had both changed and grown since those days, both in stature and in knowledge of their duties and responsibilities that lay ahead. This was the breathing space, now they stood at the bend of the river, not looking back so much as forward to a destiny that would never become a burden because henceforth she had someone, very dear and close to her, with whom to share its manifold complexities.

When they reached Birkhall, the modest retreat near Balmoral, for the second part of their honeymoon, they had an even greater sense of happy solitude, of belonging for the moment only to each other. For early that December in Scotland snow fell heavily, and there is nothing more evocative than such a white, erasing mantle outside for making any couple within the peaceful circle of the fire to feel that they really and truly are the only two people in the world.

Of course, the interlude could not last for ever. They would not have wished it, anyway. On the eve of their wedding, the King had admitted Lieutenant Mountbatten, R.N. to the Royal Family, by making him a Knight Companion of the Order of the Garter, and authorizing him to use the appellation of "Royal Highness" that he had surrendered on his naturalization as a British subject.

So once again he was Prince Philip, though no longer of Greece and Denmark. Instead, the King bestowed upon him the Dukedom of Edinburgh which had originally been created in 1727 by George II for his heir apparent, Prince Frederick, who did not, however, live to wear the crown. Becoming extinct in 1834, the dukedom was revived again in 1866 for Queen Victoria's second son, Alfred, the "sailor prince" who died, without an heir, at the turn of the century.

Now, felicitously, this particular Dukedom, reserved for members of the Royal Family, had passed to another prince who was himself every inch a sailor and determined, despite the exhausting new timetable that his marriage would entail, to continue as long as he could with his own naval career that meant everything to his manhood and his self-respect.

For obvious reasons, the Duke could not go back at once to sea, so a compromise was effected. He was posted temporarily to the Admiralty, and early in the New Year, he took up his post there, working from nine to six, except on Saturdays, when he would be free at one. Most mornings, if it was fine, he would walk down the Mall to his job, and in the late afternoon his bride of a few weeks would impatiently stand at the windows of their apartments, awaiting his return, and the sight of his figure walking through the gates, or driving past the policeman in his battered sports car.

His pay at this time as a naval lieutenant was not very lordly. Including the usual marriage allowance, and the extra three and twopence a day that he would receive for feeding himself, as he was "billeted out" he still was not earning as much as most factory workers. That is how it goes in the Services.

True, he was luckier than any of his fellow officers, in that, after a considerable debate, he had been granted an allowance of ten thousand pounds a year by Parliament to enable him to live up to his new position as consort to the future Queen of England. However, those who rolled that sum round their mouths so enviously seemed quite oblivious to the fact that what was not swallowed up by income tax would quickly be absorbed by public subscriptions and public expenses.

It was the same with the forty thousand a year provided by the Civil List for the Princess. It sounds an enormous sum, until one breaks it down under the many headings for which it has to provide.

What's more, the young couple started earning their keep the moment that they returned from their honeymoon. No grand tour of Europe, as other royal honey-

Off to Greece. Her escort is Sir John Eddelsten, who was then Commander-in-Chief of the Mediterranean Fleet

nooners had been able to indulge in, in he past. Like all British citizens, they must keep within their narrow foreign exchange allowance: and like many other young freshly married people, too, they found themselves without a home of their own, and compelled to go on living, for the present, with the bride's parents.

It was a source of great disappointment to them, indeed, a great shock, when during their honeymoon, they heard the news that the country house in which they had hoped to live, Sunninghill Park, a mile away from the Ascot Race Course, had been burnt to the ground; in fact, hopelessly gutted.

In a way, it was a personal shock to myself, when I saw the news in the morning papers, because I had stayed there so many times as the guest of its previous owners, Mr. and Mrs. Philip Hill. The property had possessed everything to make the weekends of the new owners happy, and would have been perfect for children with its private park, and its very English lawns stretching down to the side of its own lake, whose verge is massed with a magnificent show of rhododendrons every spring.

Now the golden stone façade was gone, perhaps for ever, and many people whispered that the fire, so unexpected, so unexplained, was the result of arson, a Communist plot, a wanton act of destruction aimed at the security that today surrounds the British throne.

Princess Elizabeth was deeply upset by these rumours and suggestions and tried hard not to believe them. "But people are always so kind to us," she protested, and with reason, for everywhere she and her husband went that spring, they received a tumultuous welcome. Especially was this so in Paris, when the Duke and Duchess of Edinburgh accepted an invitation from the President to pay a five-day visit at Whitsun, and open an Exhibition of Eight Centuries of British Life.

For their visit of five days they stayed at the British Embassy, and Norman Hartnell designed a special group of dresses for the Princess to wear, more sophisticated than her wedding trousseau, more in keeping with the legend that her mother had created during her own State visit to France in 1939.

But in one respect she even excelled her mother. She spoke the most idiomatic French with a perfect accent, and this enchanted her hosts, who found her the best ambassadress ever sent to their country while the crowds, as they drove through the city in an open car on their way to lay a wreath on the tomb of the Unknown Soldier, took the handsome young couple so splendidly matched in looks and bearing completely to their hearts, christening her "La Belle Princesse."

None seeing her that day, looking like a princess out of a fairy book, could guess the secret that only her husband knew. But as she went forward to lay the wreath, he watched her with a new protective tenderness. Which was indeed fortunate, for the next second she had begun to sway, and might have fallen and fainted, had he not swiftly taken her arm, and held her strongly as they made their way back to the car.

Very soon after their return from Paris an official announcement was issued from Buckingham Palace: "Her Royal Highness the Princess Elizabeth, Duchess of Edinburgh, will undertake no public engagements after the end of June."

Inside the Palace, where the young couple must continue to live until they had a home of their own, the same preparations were being made that happen at such a moment in other households, all over the world.

First the pram, last used when Alah had taken out Princess Margaret for her daily airing in the Park, was searched for, dis-

Arrival at Sagana Lodge, their wedding present from the people of Kenya

Princess Elizabeth and the Duke of Edinburgh arrive at the new African Maternity Hospital on the outskirts of Nairobi

overed at Windsor and brought out of
onourable retirement. Of course, it was an
ld-fashioned affair, but it had a great
entimental appeal for the mother-to-be,
vho was determined that all it needed was
oing-up to make it quite perfect to yet
nother generation.

As soon as it had been renovated, the
ram was constantly in demand. If the
ride was not getting her own hand in,
ushing it up and down the corridor out-
ide her apartments with Bo-Bo, her per-
onal maid, in close attendance, then Princess
Margaret was demanding her right, as a
ear-future aunt, to have a turn, too.

Next, there was the cot, where the baby
vould lie indoors. Tactfully this was re-
urbished in a colour scheme of buttercup-
ellow silk, since in this respect the Royal
'amily do not follow the usual tradition of
lue for a boy, pink for a girl. What's more,
he mother on this occasion, was firmly
n approval.

"Why, fancy a little girl turning up,"
he exclaimed to her former governess,
till her closest confidante, "and finding the
vrong-coloured cot waiting for her. Think
of her feelings. Besides, this way," she added
ruthfully, "none can guess what we are
eally hoping for ourselves."

To which Crawfie replied. "Do you remember when you were small, and used to
ay you would have lots of babies . . . two
girls and two boys, at least?"

The Princess nodded happily. She had no
ears, no doubts, during the months of
vaiting. Right up to the last she was moving
bout freely, living a full life within her own
amily circle. Only once did she put her
oot down, amid all the preparations. This

happened when it was suggested that to
ensure quiet for herself and the baby, she
should move over to a suite of apartments
on the other side of the Palace, overlooking
the lake and gardens. "I want my baby to
be born in my own room, among the things
I know," she protested.

And so, on November 14th, 1948, it
came to pass. This time there was no Home
Secretary present in the next room, as had
happened at her own birth twenty-two years
ago. This "archaic practice" was to be
discontinued, the King had announced a
fortnight previously. Instead, the telephone
would be used to inform Mr. Chuter Ede.
While as for the crowds, waiting in silent
speculation in the darkness outside the
railings, suddenly a door opened, releasing
a beam of light. One of the footmen, in his
uniform of dark blue, came out and spoke
to a policeman, who, with unaccustomed
speed, hurried towards the Palace gates.

"It's a Prince." The joyful tidings passed
over the heads of the crowd, gathering
momentum as it went. "It's a Prince."
Then the exultant whisper turned to cheering, as if the fact that the first-born was a
boy had some magical significance, some
special alchemy that was the answer to all
our troubles as a nation.

Five minutes later there was another
symbol of reassurance for the spectators. A
large Daimler came towards the crowd at
the gates, from the direction of Marlborough
House. Queen Mary was on her way to
see her first great-grandchild, later to be
christened Charles Philip Arthur George,
whose own tiny hands would one day hold
a sceptre in their grasp.

Thus that dark November night, almost

Once again she embarks, this time for an official tour of the Channel Isles

a year after the wedding, the people rejoiced once more because the direct succession to the throne was now made doubly secure. As for the mother of the babe, when she opened her eyes to look up at the fair young man leaning over her so solicitously, dressed in the grey flannels and open shirt that he had been wearing, time-killing, in the squash court, she was wrapped in a deep oblivion of peace and proud contentment.

The first milestone of their journey together had been safely reached.

CHAPTER SIX

ON Independence Day, July 4th, 1949—which seemed at the time a most suitable and symbolic date—the Duke and Duchess of Edinburgh moved from Buckingham Palace into their own home at last.

True, they hadn't had to wait as long as many newlyweds, but it had seemed long enough. However, now they were installed in Clarence House, they expected and hoped to be allowed to stay there for many years, even as the princess's parents had expected and hoped when they themselves first took over a renovated No. 145 Piccadilly.

Of course, Buckingham Palace must always remain a palace, full of marble and marble is a cold surface to touch, while the other two houses, considerable mansions though they were, could always, through the personality of their occupants, possess the warmth and atmosphere of home.

Moreover, at Clarence House, Prince Philip's wife was looking forward to leading the life of a young married woman, on her own. It is true that there are many more

beautiful town houses, from an architectural point of view, to be found in London than this one: many even larger ones, too. Neither consideration mattered at that moment in the eyes of its fresh occupants. After all, Clarence House possessed a history and a tradition as a Royal residence, while the new Duke and Duchess of Edinburgh were young enough and determined enough to banish the ghosts and gloom of disuse with children's laughter and to make a real home for themselves where it would be easy to relax during their few free moments together. A home that would be light and airy after all the dark wallpapers and the heavy Victorian furniture of the Victorian age: full of flowers and windows, and with the impression of being a house in the country.

One can argue that such a transformation should have been easy enough with a grant of fifty thousand pounds from Parliament to be administered by the Ministry of Works. In actual fact, the major part of this sum was needed for the installation of a modern lighting, heating and hot water system.

In any case, the mere spending of money does not make for a home, or create the combination of a simple good taste, with the friendly, lived-in atmosphere that Clarence House possessed at the moment when its new owners, reluctantly, had to leave it for the vast corridors—and the vast silences —of Buckingham Palace again.

The Duke's greatest delight had been his fully equipped miniature cinema in the basement, while his wife had never tired of telling her visitors that entertaining, compared with Buckingham Palace and its acres of kitchens, had been enormously

*She broadcasts in French to our
friends across the Channel*

*The Duke and Duchess of Edinburgh
arrive at the Opera House*

simplified by the introduction of the latest type of hot-plate container erected close to the service hatch for the dining-room.

To pour out such domestic details with delight is typical of our young Queen's straightforward approach to life, which was clearly defined, again, in her own personal sitting-room at Clarence House, which, despite the delicacy of its pale aquamarine walls and curtains, its exquisite Chinese carpet and blue and scarlet screen, above all, its very feminine shiny chintz covers of pink and white hollyhocks, had at the window overlooking the Park a most busi-

nesslike Chippendale writing desk of an almost masculine strength.

For the Queen never forgot when she lived there, that though this was the most beautiful room in her first married home, it was also her working room, and that it was at that same desk, facing the four framed pictures of her husband and the others of her mother and grandmother, that she had to make the decisions about her public life that must so often take her away from home, and the privacy of her own family setting.

Of course, the inexorable moving-on process means that now she is Queen,

Laughter in Boys' Town in Rome

Prince Philip's wife can never sit in that room again as chatelaine. However, no doubt she will reproduce its colour schemes in her new boudoir. In any case, I do not consider it either wasted time or space to describe in some detail what was her personal background in Clarence House, and her own fixed timetable, when in residence, since together they provide such an insight into the character of this young wife and mother who so soon now is to be crowned Elizabeth the Second.

When she is in the capital, it has been the habit of the Princess who is now our Queen to be at her desk by nine o'clock in the morning, however late her official engagements the evening before may have been, and there she has stayed until twelve—when she goes, if possible, to the children—with her secretary—then Lt.-Colonel Charteris, now Sir Alan Lascelles—and her diary at her elbow, answering letters and pencilling in the dates of her future appearances, often more than six months ahead.

Elizabeth's first instinct has always been to accept the ceaseless requests for the bounty of her presence, rather than to refuse, even though, if she turned her head away

A Royal Princess from another country pays a solemn visit to the Vatican

from her diary for a moment, it was to see on another table against the wall of her sitting-room at Clarence House, underneath the picture of "Le Lac des Cygnes", by Oliver Messel, a large picture of Prince Charles, taken at his christening. Or, on a fine day, below her window, his happy figure, in a scarlet coat, gambolling on the grass.

This sturdy small boy, who is growing to look more like his father every day, did not hold dominion for long alone over the Clarence House nurseries, since a year had hardly elapsed after the Edinburghs moved in before another baby was born to share his solitary state. This time it was a girl, weighing six pounds exactly at birth, and bringing great joy to her parents, who had hoped so eagerly that they were right to think up the names in advance, of Anne Elizabeth Alice Louise.

The little Princess came into the world, not like her brother, at night, but at ten minutes to twelve on an August morning. The Queen Mother had arrived to be near at hand, exactly five minutes before the child was born, while Prince Philip was fortunately there in time, too, having flown home on foreign service leave from Malta.

The Duke had seen little of his family for a year, ever since that day the previous October when he had left London to go back to sea and take up his posting as first lieutenant of the destroyer *Chequers*. In one way, it had been a hard decision to make, in another way a very happy one. After two years of the kind of public life his wife has to lead, Prince Philip felt that he must have a moving deck under his feet again

for a while, and become an anonymous member—Jimmy the One—of his own Service once more.

His wife understood. She had seen how thin and drawn her husband had become in London. Besides, had she not promised on her wedding day both to honour and obey? And this was a longing deep down in the roots of his being, whose fulfilment he would be able to remember with satisfaction in the long years ahead.

The very morning after he flew out to Malta in one of the Vikings of the King's Flight, his wife had started once again her round of public engagements, addressing the annual meeting of an Institution which likewise had its roots in the very heart of the country. That day, to the vast concourse of upturned faces, the Queen spoke words which would have had great significance and shown great moral courage at any time, particularly at that moment, considering the juxtaposition of the two dates in her diary:

October 17, 1949: Prince Philip leaves for Malta.

October 18, 1949: Mothers' Union meeting at Central Hall, Westminster.

This is what she said that afternoon:

"When we see around us the havoc which has been wrought, above all among the children, by the break-up of homes, we can have no doubt that divorce and separation are responsible for some of the darkest evil in our society today. I do not think that you can perform any finer service than to help to maintain the Christian doctrine that the relationship of husband and wife is a permanent one, not lightly to be broken by difficulties or quarrels."

She gives her hand in friendship to a great statesman

And then the Queen added something which, I can't help feeling, gives a deep insight into her own character. "*I believe that there is a great fear in our generation of being labelled as priggish.*" By that she meant, as she went on to explain, that people today are often afraid to show disapproval of what they know in their hearts to be wrong, and thus end up by seeming to condone what fundamentally they dislike. "*I am sure,*" she ended up, "*it is just as wrong to err on one side as it is to be intolerant and over-critical.*"

A brave declaration of faith, which shows

WEEK-END OCCASIONS

Yachting with her husband off the Cornish Coast

Waiting for her husband to bat for the Windsor Great Park team

Spectators together at a village cricket match in which the Prince made seven runs

FANNY ROSA

At the Flower Ball. Prince Charles'
mother receives a present for him

in the Mediterranean, first in H.M.S. *Chequers* and later commanding his own frigate, H.M.S. *Magpie*, his wife had to make the same very difficult decision. Should she remain with her children or fly out to join her husband from time to time in Malta?

In doing so, she would only be following the precedent of a multitude of other naval wives who in peace time take up their residence in a Valetta hotel or apartment and wait philosophically for the brief moments when their husband's ship is anchored in harbour and there is shore leave to be had. The King's daughter knew that, of course, but who needed her most? Her babies or her husband.

Of course, it wasn't such an absolute choice as that. She could compromise by flying out for a few weeks whenever her own diary permitted. This is what she did, though in some quarters she received, on her third visit, ill-founded criticism for leaving her children solely in the hands of nurses.

But what supremely capable hands! And what harm could possibly come to the children in their mother's absence? In any case, it was her own doctors who, alarmed at the determination of their royal patient to resume her public duties too soon after the birth of her second child, her almost over-zealous conscientiousness which is so much part of her make-up today, urged her to spend part of that winter in Malta. In short, she was under doctors' orders to do so. And even a year later, Princess Anne was still too young to differentiate much between the grown-ups who bent over her cot, or to notice that there was one less temporarily in her entourage.

clearly the influence and strength of her early upbringing, and also the influence and presence of someone else in her life. Her Comptroller at that time, General Sir Frederick Browning, who, instead of the pretty pattern of platitudes that has always served on Royal occasions, in the past, was eager that the Princess—as she still was—now the spokeswoman for a whole generation, should always say something vivid and true and above all, constructive, in her speeches. Which she not only does more and more, but leads the way herself by living up to her personal opinions, publicly expressed, in her own life.

Nevertheless, during the two years of her husband's absence abroad with the Fleet

*Accompanied by Countess Mountbatten of Burma,
she compliments Anna Neagle and Michael Wilding*

Whereas it meant all the difference for
the children's father to have his wife waiting
for him every time he was able to come
ashore. He could show her his own ship
now: he could show her off with equal
pride to his fellow-messmates, not as the
King of Britain's daughter, but as the girl
with whom he had fallen in love when
he had come on leave to Windsor in the
war.

On shore, they lived at the Villa Guardamangia, that had been leased by the Prince's
uncle, Earl Mountbatten of Burma, himself
returned to his first and last love, the sea.
The house on one side, looks out on to a
narrow teeming street, and its visitor loved

*Wearing the Royal Stuart tartan sash
she dances a quick-step
at the Aboyne Hall in Aberdeenshire*

the informality of her new life. She would wander about the town, sight-seeing with a scarf tied round her head: she would have her hair done in the local hairdressers, taking her turn with other Service wives: sometimes at the week-ends, when the Duke could join her, they would go dancing in the public rooms at an hotel, enjoying their Saturday evening outing.

Indeed, she enjoyed herself so much that even on one occasion, when her plane was compelled to turn back to Nice, and she stayed the night in the Hotel Negresco, her instinctive reaction was: "I'm glad of the chance to stay over."

For that unexpected delay in her journey home gave her the opportunity for a two-hour drive round Monte Carlo, and alon *Le Moyen Corniche,* to catch a glimpse c all that beauty of that southern coastlin that she might never view again, excep like so many of her future subjects, upon th screen of a cinema.

Yet everything looks so different when yo actually see it, in the flesh, and can stretc out your hand to touch the mimosa trees Up till the time of these Continental visit the girl born to be Queen had never se foot outside British soil, except for a brie official visit to Paris. So who could blame he for longing, while she was still young, an before the Palace gates shut inexorabl behind her, to see something of Europe an the way of life of other people in foreign lands

Her working desk

Clarence House, her first married home

But if there had been uninformed criticism
a small section of the Press at home about
ese private visits to her husband, when her
ildren had to be left in the care of nurses,
ere was certainly none in the Italian
pers when the Duke and Duchess of
dinburgh paid a visit to Rome in the spring
1951.

On the contrary. A wave of emotion
gulfed this pair of glitteringly good-looking
mbassadors, and the scars of war were
ally healed, first when they visited Boys'
own, where there were a thousand orphans
—the victims of Mussolini's lust for power—
d the children, dressed in their Sunday
its, would not let the beautiful lady go on
r way; and secondly, when they stood,
silent communion, after they had laid a

wreath upon the lonely windswept shores of
the British Cemetery at Anzio.

In the picture that commemorates that
pilgrimage, it would seem to me that they
represent the youth of the whole world,
praying for peace in the future, for their
children, and other generations as yet unborn.

It was with this feeling in their hearts
that they came to be received by the Pope
in private audience. The man with such
power over so many millions came to the
threshold of his study to welcome his visitors,
one dressed in naval uniform, the other
completely in black, with a veil of lace over
her head. She did not bend to kiss the ring
on his hand, as other privileged pilgrims;
instead, as they shook hands, he said: "You
are very welcome, my dear."

NOW THEIR CHILDREN
COME UPON THE SCENE

*She takes her place as the central
figure at the Trooping the Colour*

Another head of another great state, but this time the secular head, was to use that same form of address: "Thank you, my dear", when he welcomed the future Queen of England to Washington, but that long and strenuous programme was still some months away over the horizon. Here in Italy, it was still the spring and they were free for a brief while to make their own itinerary, to mingle with the other anonymous sightseers in Florence, and wander in the afternoon sun upon the Fiesole hills overlooking the city.

I know myself what an enchanted place Florence is in April, so that I can imagine so well what the reactions of the Royal tourist must have been when she saw the great baskets of carnations and freesias banked against the grey stone bridges across the Arno. And outside the city the olive trees silhouetted against a sky that was the blue of Our Lady's robe, in one of the masterpieces in the Uffizi Gallery.

One morning, as Prince Philip and his wife were paying a visit to that famous gallery, moving from room to room at their own pace, a fellow-countrywoman, recognizing them, dropped a curtsy as they passed. At once Princess Elizabeth stopped and spoke, to discover that this instinctive mark of loyal respect had come from someone who was on her honeymoon.

What a chord that must have struck in the Princess's own heart! For was not this almost a second honeymoon for themselves? Not in the December snows of Scotland this time, but in the warmth and amid all the colour of the south. A respite that they would often recall in the years ahead when they looked through the book of snapshots

Vancouver greets her Royal Visitors

at they had taken of each other smiling the sun.

Soon the captain of the *Magpie* must go ack to duty and his ship: soon his wife ust return to England and her public uties, too. Now for these few days they truly elonged to themselves.

Why, even the dance given in their honour t the British Embassy in Rome had taken n a more informal air than is usual on these ccasions. Many of the young Italian noble-en who had been invited knew nothing the intricacies of the "Eightsome Reel" nd "The Dashing White Sergeant", but ey were eager to try their luck, especially hen they were fortunate enough to find emselves dancing opposite the radiant eauty in a tiara in whose honour they had en summoned that evening. Indeed, in is eagerness to be noticed, one young man ied so hard to master the new steps that fell flat on the floor at his partner's et.

One can imagine his confusion and morti-cation as sheepishly he picked himself up. ut at once the situation was saved and his ride soothed by his partner's smiling com-ent: "Please don't apologize, because I ought I had tripped you, and it was *my* ult."

Of course he would remember that cident always, her graciousness and her glowing look of happiness that night. Just as those of us who had the good fortune to see the Princess on her return to England, take her father's place at the Trooping the Colour, will not easily forget how our future Queen looked that day in her scarlet tunic, riding on her favourite horse, Winston.

I have already described in the first

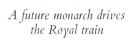

School children line the platform
at Edson in Alberta

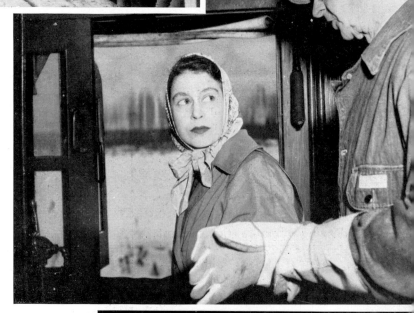

A future monarch drives
the Royal train

After her first glimpse of Canadian
Football, she greets the captains of
Winnipeg and Edmonton

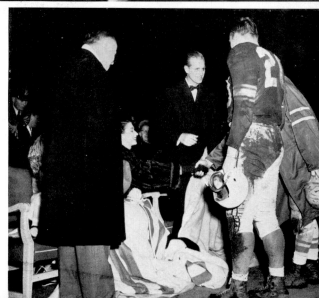

hapter how there was a new poise, a new ense of assurance about her bearing that ay, which was later to be acclaimed hroughout the North American Continent. That June morning in Whitehall it had othing to do with the precision of the parade, r her own magnificent uniform and tri-orne hat. For the same impression came to me whenever I was at one of the Princess's ublic or private appearances that summer.

Had she been dieting to make her figure uddenly so elegant, or was it the new, larker colours that she was beginning to wear, especially in the evening? These were the questions that everyone was asking. Our future Queen was certainly thinner in the face, too. But it suited her, for with her rose complexion it gave her a faint air of fragility that was immensely becoming. Moreover, she seemed to be wearing her clothes with a charming, almost Parisian air of confidence, as though for the first time she was really conscious of what a difference exactly the right dress can make to anyone's appearance.

I decided that there was none better to

The Mounties visit their Princess

discuss these changes with—as I put the finishing touches to my own portrait—than the Royal dressmaker, Norman Hartnell, and I found his words so illuminating that I will repeat them in his own words.

"When I made Her Royal Highness's first party dress just at the end of the war," he said, "she accepted the fitting as part of her official duties, but one did not feel that she was really interested in clothes as such or in creating or even following the latest fashions. Certainly not to the same degree as Princess Margaret has always been right from the start.

"Instead, Princess Elizabeth," he continued, "was happiest, one felt, in country tweeds and very simple things, and always would be. In fact, I still sensed that right up to the moment when Her Royal Highness was choosing her wedding trousseau. She was delighted, I think, with the results, and most kind to me personally, as she is to every member of my staff who has the privilege of coming in close contact with her, but at that time she made few positive suggestions, except to ask me for several dresses in her favourite lime green."

I could understand so well all that he was telling me. Everything in her mind at that moment was dedicated to the tremendous challenge ahead of her: the consciousness of it consumed her being: what she wore when she was on show in front of the people to whom she now belonged, was simply part of her answer to that challenge. For the moment, there was nothing personal about it; about all the dressing-up, that is to say.

And then something happened. Her own husband started making spontaneous com-

ments. "I like you in that dress," he might exclaim. Or "That colour suits you. Wh[y] don't you repeat it for the next tour?"

"You ask me," Norman Hartnell con[tinued, "whether Her Royal Highness ha[s] been dieting, at the Duke's suggestion. [I] know that has been freely stated, but it i[s] nonsense. I can tell you in four word[s] what has given the Princess her presen[t] figure that it is such a joy for me to dres[s] A diet of duty. That's all."

A diet of duty . . . it was a striking phras[e] and I could see very well on what m[y] informant based it. For when one consider[s] how this designer who really has the righ[t] to call himself *the* Royal dressmaker ha[s] created no fewer than eighty dresses for th[e] Canadian visit, and many for the, no[w] postponed till 1954, tour of the Antipode[s] one cannot help being conscious of all th[e] different occasions on which they would b[e] worn, and the effort entailed in the wearing A diet of duty. . . .

So many different dresses, but never [a] dummy inside. That was the ultimate test the final proof of the kind of person thi[s] second Elizabeth is, I decided, when I sa[t] by myself in a cinema and watched th[e] enchanted—for it was enchanted—film i[n] colour of the Royal visit to Canada las[t] autumn.

I had no inkling then—how could [I] have?—that so soon this young couple snatching a few days' holiday in the Keny[a] bush, would be compelled to return, wearin[g] such different clothes from the bright frock of the sunshine and the flannels of off-dut[y] hours. A diet of duty—even more onerou[s] now than either the Canadian or th[e] Australian tour that for the moment cannot b[e]

Corporal Charles Wilson
receives a present
he will treasure all his life

State Dinner at Ottawa

With Toronto's 48th Highlanders, including Master Leonard Ogben, aged four　　　*The Dionne Quins*

The Royal visitors look out over the Citadel of Quebec

Niagara Falls

*A lesson in square-dancing
in Ottawa*

Calgary stampede in a snowstorm ▶

*Two symbolic figures of the English-Speaking World have their
photograph taken together in Washington*

But what is the most remarkable quality of all in our new Queen is her capacity for performing her public duties, wherever she goes, with the dignity of a veteran at the job and yet the grace and charm of a young bride. She makes it all seem fresh and natural and so very real: the spontaneity of her smiling, her arm uplifted in the Royal salute she first had instituted in her by Alah, her nanny, when she was still a baby; above all, her handshake multiplied hundreds and hundreds of times as she crossed the North American Continent, from east to west, west to east.

Never once did her step falter, never once did her forehead set in a frown, her mouth droop. I do not make that statement simply from sitting in a darkened cinema watching a film that has been carefully edited into a work of art as well as a footnote to history. No, I speak with confidence because of all that I have heard from those whose business it was to shadow this Royal figurehead at

every moment during her final tour as Princess Elizabeth.

There was, for instance, the day when the Royal ambassadress was due to tour a Toronto hospital. And what a day it was for a boy of sixteen, Paul Mitchell, a cripple who could not leave his bed but spent the hours waiting, adjusting his camera. He was determined to get the best pictures in Toronto.

But then, as so often happens when the great moment came, something went wrong. His flash-gun refused to function. The Queen paused, wanting to help; a keen photographer herself, who understood so well his over-anxious zeal of the moment. As Paul tried to hide his emotions, the Princess walked over to his bed and exclaimed: "Never mind, I will come back before I go. I promise."

And she did, and Paul got his picture.

Then there was the day when the Royal train stopped at a far-off level crossing in Ontario. That was always happening. In

The Verger of Washington Cathedral has rather special visitors

Carefree arrival in Kenya   *Peace for a moment*

some tiny wayside station, at all hours of the day and night, the people would gather in the hopes that it might happen . . . the future Queen would show herself to her father's people, so that all their life they would have that memory of someone so far removed from them and yet so close to them in ties of loyalty and a destiny shared by every member of the Commonwealth.

So when the train came to an unscheduled standstill that morning in Ontario, it was to find five families optimistically standing beside the line waving Union Jacks. Whereupon, out of the car where she was sitting, down on to the track, stepped the girl whose name at this moment is on everyone's lips. "Hallo, what a nice day it is," she said, adding with the smile which lights up her

whole face and makes her look so defencelessly young. "Do you want to see Prince Philip? He has gone up to the front. He wants to drive the train to Hamilton and we don't have the chance to do these things at home."

Prophetic words indeed. Now one can look at the pictures of that tour in a fresh light. Does not the Queen's face take on a new radiance when one catches her delight in learning square-dancing at the special party given for her by the Governor-General? When they boarded the train again at midnight, both the Queen and her husband were still wearing the bright, informal clothes—the blue jeans, the cotton skirt—in which they had danced with all the abandon of their youth.

The sad return

How wise they had been to snatch what moments of informal relaxation they could! When they returned from Canada, everyone remarked on how fined-down the King's elder daughter looked in her pictures. Was she over-taxing her strength? It was announced that she would rest as much as she could up till the Australian tour, and anyway she would have the complete break in the Kenya sunshine, and in the privacy of the delightful bungalow that was the one wedding present she had not yet seen.

On the afternoon of their departure, I myself happened to be taking tea with the housekeeper of Windsor Castle. It was a private visit to a woman of great sensibility.

Mrs. Bruce is a Scot, like the Queen Mother, and has been in the family's service for so many years that it is not surprising her sitting-room should be filled with mementoes and pictures of the girl who was Princess Elizabeth, ever since she was a baby in her mother's arms.

Later my hostess conducted me on a personal tour of the Royal apartments, which was a very moving experience for me, especially when I found myself standing in the room that had been the children's schoolroom throughout the war years.

Now, of course, everything was under dust covers, and with the early winter dusk pressing against the windows, I had a sense of ghostly figures outside upon the terrace, a sense of sudden oppression only dissipated by the warm, Scottish voice of my companion. She was saying.

"Of course, I have many memories of those days, but the one which I think will always be my own favourite happened one evening when His Majesty had been broadcasting towards the end of the war. After listening to the King's voice myself, I had gone to the Princess's apartments to see that everything was all right for the night.

"I could not help remarking to Her Royal Highness what a wonderful broadcast it had been, and she smiled that lovely smile when her whole face lights up and said: 'Yes, it was wonderful, Mrs. Bruce. I can't listen to anything more tonight. As soon as I have fed the dogs I am going out on to the terrace to think about it by myself'."

I did not imagine as I drove away that afternoon from the castle which for centuries now has stood as a symbol of the strength of our monarchy that within a few days I would be compelled to contrast in my mind the picture of a schoolgirl in her teens, so moved by her father's voice on the radio with that other picture of the daughter wakened, if not from actual sleep, then from her holiday mood, to be told that she would never hear that voice again.

Yet on her last evening together in London all their talk had been of how her parents, too, would soon be going for a holiday cruise. So much was expected from that, and no doubt during that happy family party when they all went to Drury Lane to see *South Pacific* they must have admitted to each other how desperately they looked forward to escaping, even for a brief time, from the inexorable winter cold into sunshine, into summer.

Alas, it could not be. The rest already is history. When, summoned back from her happy, carefree respite in the flowering wilderness of the Kenya bush, that figure, now in black, stepped once more on to the tarmac of London airport, it was to see not the bare-headed figure of her father waving to her, but the Prime Minister of England, his head uncovered, to offer obeisance to Elizabeth the Second.

Apart from the overpowering weight of her sorrow, did she feel a different person as her car turned out of the gates of London airport from the girl whose story I have been telling from the day of her birth, and who had driven the other way, only a week ago? One cannot answer such questions, one can only surmise—and surely she had been prepared for this moment for a long time—but as I cut out those last pictures for the scrapbook I have always kept, or perhaps the first ones for the new story just

Dorothy Wilding

First Command Portrait of the young Queen's reign

beginning to unfold, I was suddenly conscious once more of the day that I had sat in King George VI's sitting-room at Buckingham Palace, so that a lady-in-waiting should tell me all that she could about the young girl who was nicknamed Lilibet.

For she was then Lilibet still. And I heard—do you remember—of the morning, nearly ten years ago, when Lilibet drove from Windsor to Salisbury Plain to make her first appearance at a parade of the Battalion of Guards whose honorary colonel she had just become.

All through the journey her nervousness increased into such a crescendo that the lady-in-waiting took out of her bag a bar of barley sugar. It was the last of her sweet ration, but she sacrificed it that war time morning in a good cause. "I told Lilibet how good it was for her stomach muscles at such a moment" she explained.

I recounted that charming and so revealing anecdote in the first chapter, I know. But has that schoolgirl in her teens who has now become the first lady in our land forgotten that incident of long ago? I hope not, for it is a very touching memory, though certainly she has no need of such supports any longer. For she possesses already the dignity and poise of her mother, and what higher praise can one suggest than that?

However, when the Royal car drew up once more in front of the portico of Clarence House and the Princess, who had become overnight the Queen, stepped out, it was not to be greeted by her mother, who was keeping her last vigil at Sandringham, but by the oldest member of the family, its matriarchal head. It had been Queen Mary's express wish that she should be the first member of the family to pay homage.

Always before in Queen Mary's presence Elizabeth would curtsy, before being kissed warmly on her cheek. But this time it was different, this time they were on equal terms, the one who had given so much, the other who had so much still to give. As they came towards each other, it was the infinitely older woman who in a sudden obeisance, curtsied and kissed the hand of Elizabeth the Second. Whereupon a look of recognition passed between them that only they could fully understand. When King George the Fifth died, his loving wife turned from his bed to kiss the hand of her son Edward, next in the line of kings. Now it was the destiny of her granddaughter to assume the mantle, and never falter in the years ahead.

Always in the past, England has been prosperous and united under her queens. I dare to prophesy that it will be the same again, the flowering of a new Elizabethan age, for has not King George the VI's daughter already proved her quality again and again? So let us close the book, with grief and gratitude towards the monarch who never spared himself, and has now gone to his rest, but with new love and new hope towards his heir who is still so young and yet so unafraid.

After Queen Victoria was crowned, she wrote in her diary. "*I feel very proud to be the queen of such a nation*". I have no doubt that I am writing for us all when I suggest that we, in our turn, feel equally proud to have this second Elizabeth as our sovereign and the defender of our faith.

Long may she reign over us. God Save the Queen.

ELIZAB